Bridge Builders

To Grandpa R.D., who embodied the essence of bridge building

Bridge Builders

Bringing People Together in a Polarized Age

———

Nathan Bomey

polity

The right of Nathan Bomey to be identified as Author of this Work has been asserted in accordance with the UK Copyright, Designs and Patents Act 1988.

First published in 2021 by Polity Press

Reprinted 2021

Polity Press
65 Bridge Street
Cambridge CB2 1UR, UK

Polity Press
101 Station Landing
Suite 300
Medford, MA 02155, USA

ISBN-13: 978-1-5095-4593-3

A catalogue record for this book is available from the British Library.

Library of Congress Cataloging-in-Publication Data
Names: Bomey, Nathan, author.
Title: Bridge builders : bringing people together in a polarized age /
   Nathan Bomey.
Description: Cambridge, UK ; Medford, MA : Polity Press, 2021. | Includes
   bibliographical references. | Summary: "An absorbing and inspiring
   portrait of individuals who are uniting divided communities across
   America"-- Provided by publisher.
Identifiers: LCCN 2020055372 (print) | LCCN 2020055373 (ebook) | ISBN
   9781509545933 (hardback) | ISBN 9781509545940 (epub)
Subjects: LCSH: Polarization (Social sciences)--United
   States--History--21st century. | United State--Social conditions--21st
   century.
Classification: LCC HN90.P57 B66 2021 (print) | LCC HN90.P57 (ebook) |
   DDC 306.0973--dc23
LC record available at https://lccn.loc.gov/2020055372
LC ebook record available at https://lccn.loc.gov/2020055373

Typeset in 11 on 13pt Sabon by
Servis Filmsetting Ltd, Stockport, Cheshire
Printed and bound in the United States by LSC Communications

For further information on Polity, visit our website:
politybooks.com

Contents

Prologue: The Better Angels of Our Nature

In many ways, America is like one big dysfunctional family that, despite its differences, is better off when it's communicating and cooperating effectively, even though we will never agree on everything. But lately we've been emotionally abusing each other, failing to listen to one another, and exploiting each other's failings.

The fact that we increasingly can't hold fruitful conversations with people who aren't like us – which is the key to finding common ground and thus achieving political, social, and cultural progress – illustrates the depths of our civic crisis. Productive discourse in spite of our disagreements is "the arch stone of democracy" – it's what holds us together – according to David Blankenhorn, cofounder of Braver Angels, a nonprofit that teaches Americans from different backgrounds how to communicate. "Conversation is the very heart and soul of self-government," Blankenhorn said. "It always has been. You can't run a democracy without that."

In view of the parallels between familial discord and our crisis of polarization, it would seem appropriate to look to family therapy for clues on how to improve our national dialogue. And that's precisely how Braver Angels got started. Originally known as Better Angels, the nonprofit was founded in the wake of the 2016 US election by a group of politically diverse Americans who were determined to catalyze healthy conversation about the issues that divide us. "Family therapy has been dealing with" polarization for as long as there has been family therapy – just in a different context – said Brookings Institution political scholar Jonathan Rauch, a former member of the Better Angels board. "Typically, when you have a marriage or family that's having problems, you're dealing with . . . strong emotional feelings, which are blocking communication, exacerbating stereotypes, [and] causing discursive loops that go in the wrong direction where people escalate."

Sounds familiar, right? That's what we see all around us.

Bill Doherty, one of the nation's leading family therapists and a cofounder of Braver Angels, designed the group's community workshops to bring together an equal number of Republicans and Democrats – or what he calls "reds" and "blues" – in small-group settings. The participants typically spend several hours immersed in a series of conversations moderated by trained volunteers to learn how to more effectively communicate with people on the other side. "So when they speak, you have to create a structure that makes it unlikely that they will go on the attack and a space that gives them an opportunity to listen to the other," Doherty said.

That approach comes directly from couples counseling, where the therapist is firmly in control of the conversation from the beginning. "You don't let them turn to each other and then start processing an argument that they had – because if they could do that on their own well, they wouldn't be paying you," Doherty said. "Careful attention is paid to minimizing the likelihood of flare-ups and meltdowns because you have trouble recovering from that."

While people are allowed to express their views in the Braver Angels workshops, they're also encouraged to examine the limitations and flaws of their own side.

This concept also comes directly from counseling strategy. "In working with couples, the real takeoff point occurs for people getting better when they see that their problems are not just due to their spouse's bad behavior or rotten personality, but they see themselves as contributors, if you will, to the polarization that has occurred," Doherty said.

From a practical perspective, Braver Angels places one group of politically like-minded people in a circle to have a conversation with each other. The participants from the opposite side of the aisle are positioned in a circle around the original group and are instructed to listen but not speak, creating the feeling of a fishbowl. The people in the inner circle are then asked to discuss their values and consider why their preferred political policies are good for the country. That gives them a chance to crow about why their side is superior.

"The second question is, 'What are your reservations or concerns about your own side?'" Doherty said. "There you get people to be self-reflective, to be self-critical, to recognize that their side doesn't have it all nailed. And there is this almost visceral softening you can feel in the room. People on the outside have exactly those criticisms. And you're not coming across as a fanatic."

Then the groups trade places. This exercise helps members of each group see that people on the other side recognize some of their own flaws and that people on both sides might have something in common. The lesson here? When you display a degree of vulnerability and humility, you can begin to make genuine connections with others.

In another exercise, the groups break off and examine negative perceptions about their respective sides, listing the most common stereotypes about them. "Typically, the reds would make lists of things like, 'We don't care about the poor,' or, 'We're a bunch of racists,' and blues will make lists like, 'We're unpatriotic,' and, 'We're all for open borders,'" Rauch said.

Each group is then asked to examine whether there's a kernel of truth in the other side's perceptions. "And people say, 'Well, racists are attracted to our side and some of our leaders are, and it's disturbing to us,'" Doherty said. It's only after these sessions, which force the participants to consider each other as human beings, that the groups begin to discuss hot-button issues directly with each other.

Braver Angels has achieved extraordinary results by teaching people how to communicate. By April 2020, the group had nearly 10,000 dues-paying members and 1,240 volunteers, including 630 moderators trained to lead sessions on their own, according to Blankenhorn. Before the coronavirus pandemic shut down in-person gatherings in early 2020, the nonprofit was conducting a total of 15 to 18 sessions per week throughout the United States. When the pandemic hit, Braver Angels temporarily switched to online sessions, holding dynamic conversations on topics ranging from the 2020 election to race relations in the aftermath of George Floyd's killing in Minneapolis. Membership more than tripled during the year.

The group's goal is to help people "see the little bit of humanity that you recognize is shared with you in the other person to the degree that you have an inner desire to do good to them, even though you disagree strongly," Blankenhorn said. "That's really all we're trying to do."

From the beginning, Braver Angels had no interest in the pursuit of political consensus among the participants. "We were not that much interested in having people agree on policy. We were not that much interested in having people adopt a centrist political philosophy. We were not that interested in getting people to modify or change their views of public policy issues. Nor were we particularly interested in having them agree on facts,"

Blankenhorn said. "Our point of view was that what one views as a fact depends on questions of social trust, not the facticity of the fact."

Without reestablishing social trust, we've got no hope of getting on the same page. "The diminishment of social trust was the reason that we believe that people couldn't agree on facts," Blankenhorn said. "So what we were trying to do was establish social trust, which we believe is a precondition for all these other things."

Doherty said Americans won't get on the same page until they recognize that everyone must be part of the solution – just like for couples to be successful in therapy, both people must embrace the role they can play in pursuit of relational reconciliation. "It has to be a *we* problem, not just a *you* problem," said Doherty, who is also a former president of the National Council on Family Relations. "And if *we* have a problem, then more of us may have some motivation to try to be curious and understand the other side."

Doherty recalled that after one Braver Angels session, one group member walked away with the transformational realization that he was part of the problem – much like drivers complain about congestion: "This person realized, '*I am traffic*.'"

Yet even if the entire nation entered into the political version of family therapy, we'd still struggle with the purely human magnetism of polarization. It will never go away in full. But that doesn't mean we can't find common ground more often. "I tell people at the end of successful couples therapy that you are now much more aware of the handful of problems that you will have until death do you part," Doherty said, only half joking. "Hopefully what you've gotten from this is better understanding of [those problems] and better ways to deal with them, having them be annoyances rather than life threatening – and to live gracefully and graciously with them."

Clearly, we can't send everyone in the United States to Braver Angels workshops. We need a more realistic approach to helping people find common ground within the context of their daily lives. But what Braver Angels has proven, within the confines of a civic laboratory, is that reestablishing social trust is possible when approached strategically.

So how do we go about it in real life?

Since you've picked up this book, you are at least curious about the possibility that there are proven methods for bringing people together despite their differences. But perhaps you are skeptical. You're thinking, Americans are stubborn and won't change their minds no matter what we try.

Maybe you're right. Maybe our divides are too wide to be bridged. I can't rule it out. Yet if history is our guide, there is hope.

Take it from Rauch and Blankenhorn. During the early 2000s, they engaged in a years-long debate about the merits of gay marriage. Blankenhorn, who is straight, actively opposed it, while Rauch, who is gay, was a vocal proponent and had written a book about it. "We went at it hammer and tong as intellectual adversaries," Rauch said.

There was no reason to believe they'd ever find common ground on one of the most contentious political topics in America at the time. But as they got to know each other – as their friendship deepened and they engaged in an ongoing conversation about the issue – Blankenhorn eventually came over to Rauch's side. His change of heart on marriage equality ultimately led him down a path to the creation, in 2016, of Better Angels. "I changed my mind on gay marriage mostly stemming from my relationship with Jonathan," Blankenhorn said. "We began in this public debate, but then we eventually became friends."

Blankenhorn's experience brought him to a realization

that the establishment of social trust is the first step toward getting on the same page. It's not enough to simply present new facts or opinions. "But because of relationships," he said, "you can change your mind and still feel that you're being true to yourself."

Introduction

When the COVID-19 pandemic erupted in early 2020, I thought perhaps this would be the catalyst that finally brought Americans together. Surely this crisis – a life-or-death situation for millions of people – would prompt us to rally alongside one another, bond with each other despite our differences, and set aside our political disagreements to get through it together.

Looking back on it, my hope was terribly naive. It didn't happen. It was never going to happen.

Yes, Americans showed plenty of support for frontline workers who put their lives at risk to contain the virus. And we did a lot of Zoom calls with our friends, which was nice for a while until it got tiresome. But it wasn't long before we began bickering over the roots of the COVID-19 crisis and arguing over what to do about it.

The tendency of some Republicans, in particular, to resist the exhortations of public health officials to wear masks placed them and others at risk of death and profound economic hardship.[1] One reason may be because then-President Donald Trump initially refused to set a good example by wearing a mask in public. To be sure, at various stages during the pandemic, many other prominent Republicans, including Ohio Governor Mike DeWine and Senate Majority Leader Mitch McConnell of Kentucky, publicly promoted masks, which were scientifically proven to save people from contracting the disease.² Nonetheless, mask wearing became so contentious that National Public Radio referred to it as "another signifier of political identity," as Republicans insistent on maintaining their personal freedom declared that masks are "for the weak" and reflect "government overreach." On the other hand, there were also reports of people – presumably Democrats in many cases – berating others for not wearing masks in socially distanced outdoor situations where they were scientifically unnecessary.³ Debate about the seriousness of the crisis even turned rigidly partisan, as Republicans became less concerned about it as the months went along, while Democrats became more concerned.⁴

We should not be surprised that the pandemic turned out to be a force of division. One-time events – no matter how significant – are no match for our chronic divisiveness. Even sudden disruption of our way of living cannot overcome the disgust we have for others who aren't like us. Such disruption can provide only a superficial sense of togetherness – and usually for a short period of time – unless people on the ground are ready, willing, and able to organically transform their circumstances into an opportunity to build bridges toward each other. Absent such a concerted effort, we'd rather fight about our circumstances than fight together against our circumstances.

It was, in fact, virtually inevitable that the pandemic – which, by the end of 2020, had killed more than 340,000 Americans, infected more than 19.6 million,⁵ and ravaged the economy – would cast a spotlight on our national divides. Much like there was no quick fix for the pandemic after it began raging, so there is no quick fix for our crisis of polarization – no treatment that can eradicate divisiveness overnight. "The divisions between Republicans and Democrats on fundamental political values – on government, race, immigration, national security, environmental protection, and other areas – reached record levels during Barack Obama's presidency," according to the Pew Research Center, and those gaps grew "even larger" under Trump.[6] During his four years in the White House, Trump personally and relentlessly attacked his political opponents, emboldened White nationalists, assailed reporters as enemies, and unleashed furious tweets day after day, among innumerable other polarizing actions and statements.

After Democratic presidential nominee Joe Biden's defeat of Trump in the November 2020 election, we can certainly hope that political polarization will ease a bit, in part because of the former vice president's pledge to pursue bipartisanship and the perception that he could serve as the "healer-in-chief" following Trump's intensely polarizing reign.[7] But Biden's win was far from the sweeping victory that might've signaled a national repudiation of Trump's style of political vengeance and intransigence. Rather, although Biden received the most votes of any presidential candidate in US history while campaigning on a platform to unify the country – more than 75 million people backed him – Trump got more votes than any previous sitting president.[8] Despite all the polarizing things he was responsible for, Trump still won the support of more than 72 million Americans on election day.[9]

And even though he outperformed expectations, Trump baselessly labeled the election results as fraudulent.[10] His own Department of Homeland Security reported that the election was "the most secure in American history,"[11] yet Trump repeatedly refused to concede. In doing so, he injected further animus into the American political environment, threatening to erode voters' confidence in future elections and further solidifying the fissures that plague our democracy.

As the election showed us, the things that divide us are deeply embedded in the American psyche. They cannot be swept away with a particular electoral outcome or erased by an inspiring politician. Among Democrats, 61 percent view Republicans as racist, bigoted, and sexist, while 54 percent of Republicans view Democrats as spiteful and 49 percent view them as ignorant, according to a poll conducted in late 2019 for digital news outlet *Axios*. About one-fifth of Democrats and one-fifth of Republicans view the other side as "evil."[12]

Yes, that's the same adjective we would typically use to characterize Maleficent from *Sleeping Beauty* or Scar from *The Lion King* – as in, the same way we would describe a maniacal sorcerer or a murderous tyrant from an animated movie. But there's nothing cinematic or fictitious about our situation. No one is here to sing "Hakuna Matata" and explain how we're all part of the circle of life.

Among both Democrats and Republicans, only 2–3 percent view the other side as kind, while no more than 4 percent view the other side as thoughtful, according to the *Axios* survey. The poll had a margin of error of three points, meaning the percentage of Democrats and Republicans who view each other as kind could be as low as zero.[13] Think about that for a second.

The tendency of people of difference to loathe one another on a deeply personal level is what political scientists call "affective polarization" – and it's coursing through America's veins. "When polarization started emerging, it looked like disagreement about issues," said Jonathan Rauch, a US political scholar at the Brookings Institution. "Affective polarization is different because it means you have an actual emotional dislike of the other side. It's often not even issue based. It's based on the sense that the other side is dangerous, evil, wants to endanger people like me – a threat."

In lawmaking, affective polarization throttles legislative progress because politicians don't have an incentive to work together if their constituents actively or passively support their obstinacy. That's obvious to anyone acquainted with the unending stasis on Capitol Hill.

Our democratic principles are at risk of crumbling if we can't have difficult conversations with people of difference, tackle challenging issues together, confront our personal biases, and see the world through each other's eyes. As conservative scholar and author Arthur C. Brooks wrote in his 2019 book, *Love Your Enemies*, affective polarization is breeding a culture of contempt. It is undermining entire communities, interpersonal relationships, and institutional stability.

In the workplace, we have an actual financial incentive to get along, yet affective polarization is still prominent. Personal contempt is leading employees to spurn others who don't share their political views. According to a study by research and advisory group Gartner, 36 percent of employees avoided talking to or collaborating with a coworker during the 2020 presidential primary season because of that colleague's political views. Nearly one-third reported that they had "witnessed at least one instance of unacceptable treatment of a coworker because of their political beliefs, including being called offensive names, being avoided by colleagues, or being treated unfairly."[14]

Before the pandemic had even begun, pervasive divisiveness had afflicted the personal lives of about one-third of Americans, of whom about four in ten had experienced depression, anxiety, or sadness because of it, according to a poll conducted in late 2019 by the nonpartisan research group Public Agenda for *USA Today*'s Hidden Common Ground project.[15]

If nothing else, COVID-19 has shown us that affective polarization can even be deadly. When we make lifestyle decisions based on tribalistic politics rather than science, we are putting the lives of the people around us at risk of contracting the virus. Yet, ironically, even if there were a vaccine to treat polarization, many Americans would refuse it. Just as a misguided slice of Americans – including a cross-section of those on both the left and the right – won't listen to the science that vaccines are safe and necessary to preserve public health,[16] many of us won't listen to the facts on other issues if those facts contradict our preconceived notions about each other and the world around us.[17]

As a newspaper journalist, I've devoted my life to seeking out the truth. So it pains me to admit that publishing the facts through old-fashioned media isn't enough to get people on the same page. The decline of traditional news media has frayed the relationship between Americans and professional journalists, whose collective bond of civic trust has been further ravaged by false accusations of "fake news" leveled at journalists from the likes of Trump and his hyperpartisan media supporters. Amid my industry's financial implosion – which has led to massive layoffs, publication shutdowns, and so-called "news deserts"[18] – social media platforms have become the new gatekeepers for the information that many people see about the world. These technology giants are enabling misinformation to flourish and profiting from it.[19]

Consequently, Americans have been largely left to fend for themselves on an information superhighway riddled with potholes of falsehoods that further divide our society. Owing to the classic psychological condition of confirmation bias, many of us believe and actively spread the lies. As falsehoods flourish, our emotions become supercharged, and our crisis of polarization worsens. And there's no reason to believe our increasingly cacophonous public discourse will suddenly become symphonic, absent a new orchestration specifically composed to achieve harmony.

William Galston – who cofounded No Labels and The New Center, groups that work to bolster the political

center in America – began studying American polarization at the Brookings Institution during the second Iraq
War. Polarization "seemed very serious back then," he
said. "It's clear in retrospect we hadn't seen anything
yet. Every year I say to myself, 'It can't get worse than
this.' And every year it gets worse."

Ensconced in our political echo chambers, we are
constantly fed the premise that the other side is crazy.
Talking heads say it. Social media says it. Politicians
say it. Even journalists say it. And Americans have
bought into it: 87 percent of Democrats and 84 percent
of Republicans say the other side is hateful, while 88
percent of Democrats and 88 percent of Republicans say
the other side is brainwashed, according to a June 2019
survey by the nonpartisan group More in Common for
its Hidden Tribes of America project.[20]

But are we truly as far apart as we feel? More in
Common, which studies political tribalism in an attempt
to bridge ideological divides, examined "second-order
beliefs" – that is, what people believe others believe. It
turns out that we may not be as polarized as we think
we are.

The study concluded that "Democrats and Republicans
imagine that almost twice as many people on the other
side hold extreme views than really do." For example,
Democrats underestimate the share of Republicans who
believe that "many Muslims are good Americans" by 29
points, and underestimate the percentage who believe
that "properly controlled immigration can be good for
America" by 33 points. Likewise, Republicans overestimate the percentage of Democrats who agree that
"the US should have completely open borders" by 33
points, and overestimate the share of Democrats who
believe that "America should be a socialist country" by
25 points.[21]

Perception, of course, is reality – so that wide gap
in second-order beliefs has become a self-fulfilling

prophecy. But that doesn't mean Americans like it this way. "After more than a decade of intensifying polarization, even people who disagree with each other pretty vehemently are hungering for a politics that feels different, politics that sounds different, politics that doesn't make us hate our neighbors," Galston said.

He's right. The Hidden Tribes project found that 67 percent of Americans constitute an "exhausted majority" containing "distinct groups of people with varying degrees of political understanding and activism" who "share a sense of fatigue with our polarized national conversation, a willingness to be flexible in their political viewpoints, and a lack of voice in the national conversation."[22]

"What is it that's exhausting people? The constant fighting. The sense that we are devoting 99 percent of our energy to struggling with each other," Galston said. "It's like this giant social war where roughly half the country is pulling hard in one direction, and roughly half the country is pulling just as hard in the other direction, and the rope isn't moving. We're getting really tired. It takes a real effort to keep on going in a tug of war, but it can get pretty frustrating if the rope never moves."

The rope is stuck in myriad ways. On immigration, for example, lawmakers have been deadlocked for at least a generation over how to handle people living in the country without legal documentation and how to handle border security. But most Americans are not divided on the issue, according to The New Center's research. "You have one party that's offering a wall and another party that seems to be offering open borders," Galston said. "Majorities don't want the wall, they don't want family separation, they don't want non-responsiveness to refugees fleeing a genuine fear of persecution. On the other hand, they don't want open borders, they don't want sanctuary cities, they don't want to abolish ICE" – the US Immigration and Customs Enforcement agency.

What most Americans want is something in the middle. But political paralysis has prevented a solution, in part because people on the far left and the far right wield so much influence over public policy debates. Progressive activists and devoted conservatives make up only 8 percent and 6 percent of Americans, respectively, despite having an outsized influence on our political discourse.[23]

"It's been a political science truism for decades now ... that intense minorities can have disproportionate effects on politics – and issues like immigration tend to attract passionate minorities on both sides," Galston said. "They set the terms of the debate within their respective parties but not in the country."

That paradigm is ensuring a political stalemate because the nation's two-party system was designed to guarantee that neither side gets what it wants in full. "The political system for too long has been guided by the hope of both political parties that they were on the verge of winning a sweeping victory that would enable them to form a new permanent governing majority and just get their way," Galston said. "Faced with compromise or stagnation, the system has elected to go down the path of stagnation."

Indeed, compromise has become an anachronism in part because there's little consequence for the engineers of stagnation. Politicians are consistently rewarded in lopsided, gerrymandered primary elections for standing their ground and refusing to budge based purely on their ideological principles. That stubbornness makes the pursuit of common ground extraordinarily difficult.

Yet our leaders won't change unless we change. Otherwise there's no incentive for them to do anything differently. And that means we need to embrace relationships and conversation with people who aren't like us. It means we need to immerse ourselves in friendships and interaction with people of difference that expose us to their perspectives and to the challenges they face, even when the process makes us uncomfortable. If we don't work with each other – if we don't build bridges – we'll never achieve progress together.

Sometimes the path to conversation, understanding, and cooperation proceeds slowly, as we gradually learn more about each other and become more attuned to the structural issues that underpin our polarized culture. And sometimes it happens swiftly, when we become viscerally aware of the need to span the gaps that have divided us for ages.

When I began working on this book in late 2018, I never imagined we would see the type of national outcry over the compounding scourge of racism that we saw in the wake of the death of George Floyd, a 46-year-old Black man, on May 25, 2020, at the hands of the police in Minneapolis. The searing sound of Floyd pleading, "I can't breathe," and crying out for his mother as White officer Derek Chauvin kneeled on his neck while he suffocated[24] shocked many White Americans into realizing for the first time that racism manifested in the form of police brutality is still real and vicious. But, perhaps even more significantly, it also shocked them into recognizing that police brutality is just one element in a much broader societal scheme that keeps Black Americans under the knees of White privilege.

The death of George Floyd was the latest in a seemingly endless series of violent acts by police against Black people – including incidents like the killing in 2014 of Michael Brown in Ferguson, Missouri, which spurred outrage among some White Americans for a while, yet eventually faded from the national spotlight. But this time, the shock factor sparked a burgeoning awareness of the need for White Americans to step out onto metaphorical ledges and to begin building bridges across structural ravines that have long prevented Black Americans from escaping the trenches of economic inequality, underfunded schools, and lack of access to adequate medical care, to mention just a few obstacles to social justice.

The national outpouring of anger following Floyd's death was largely directed at the White establishment, as Americans of all races hit the streets throughout the country to protest and demand change despite an ongoing pandemic that put their lives at risk. The groundswell of outrage can serve as the raw material for the type of bridge building that needs to be done to begin overcoming the whitecapped rapids of racism. The key will be to ensure that the protests translate into lasting bridges, which are the key to policy change. For that, White Americans, myself included, cannot ask Black people to meet us halfway. White people need to use their voices and places of privilege to speak up and take action by constructing the bridges that they have so long neglected to build.

Building bridges between people of difference against a backdrop of racism, political polarization, misinformation, and social division may sound like a milquetoast way of pursuing change. But it's not. Rather, it's a bold form of countercultural revolution. It stands in stark contrast to the typical way of doing things, in which we stand firm on our cultural biases, cling to social and political isolation, and refuse to consider the possibility that we could be wrong.

Bridge building does not, however, require unity. And it does not involve cultural assimilation. That is a false assumption. What's required is the pursuit of understanding – that is, the pursuit of social trust, as David Blankenhorn of Braver Angels described it. Social trust paves the way for structural change that can bring about tangible benefits for our society at large.

But how do we pursue social trust when the things

that divide us feel so overwhelming? How do we achieve policy progress when our polarized politics have taught us that we should never have to compromise? How do we foster improved communication to combat the crisis of misinformation that fans the flames of division? And how do we ensure that the movement that arose in the wake of George Floyd's death turns into substantive change among White Americans who previously did not grasp or care about the need to fight racism?

As I began considering ways to address polarization in this book, I figured there must be people out there who aren't accepting the status quo. There must be people who are bringing others of difference together. There must be people who are dedicating themselves to fostering dialogue, mending broken relationships, and finding common ground.

I'm here to tell you that they're out there. I visited them. I talked with them. And I believe that we can – we must – learn from them.

They are not Pollyannaish. They are not impervious to discouragement. They are not flawless.

But they are hopeful, they are driven, and they are countercultural.

They are bridge builders.

Bridge builders are people like Eboo Patel.

About a quarter century ago, racial tension was high following the police beating of Rodney King, the O. J. Simpson trial, and what Patel called "the emergence of identity politics on college campuses." "It wasn't as politically divided" as things are today, "but it was socially divided in a variety of ways," he said.

For a while, Patel was immersed in the divisiveness. "I spent a couple of years angry," he said. "And then frankly I developed some perspective and maturity and judgment. Along the way, I discovered religion."

He devoted himself to his faith as a Muslim of Gujarati Indian heritage. At the same time, he began learning more about the discordant role that religion was playing in the world, including in the assassination of Israeli Prime Minister Yitzhak Rabin and in the Yugoslav wars. But he also began learning more about what he called "the positive role that religious identity had played in social movements," such as the struggle to defeat apartheid in South Africa, the American Civil Rights Movement, and "the language used by everybody from Dorothy Day to Jane Addams to Martin Luther King, Jr., to Joshua Abraham Heschel."

Patel's personal journey gave him the conviction that "religion can be a bunker of isolation, it can be a barrier of division, it can be a bludgeon of domination, or it can be a bridge of cooperation."

That led him in the late 1990s to form the Interfaith Youth Core (IFYC) to promote conversation, relationships, and cooperation among college students from different religious backgrounds. Today, the nonprofit provides training, organizes volunteer outings, and offers curricula on interfaith issues. By April 2020, IFYC had established a presence on more than 600 campuses throughout the country with about 100,000 student participants.[25]

Patel has advocated for higher-education leaders to allay marginalization and sniping among evangelical Christians, atheists, and Muslims by integrating "conversations about religious diversity" into "first-year orientation, required courses, and policies that affect campus climate."[26]

Since Patel often finds himself attempting to bridge gaps between students from completely different worlds, I asked him whether he felt like his work was countercultural. I certainly think it is. But he disagreed – and his response was reflective of the way bridge builders tend to see the world differently. "If America is defined by

cable news, then what we're doing is countercultural,"
he said. "But if America is defined by what we do on a
regular basis in hospitals, in little leagues, in pickup basketball, in hip-hop ciphers, then it's actually very much
part of the American way."

Patel said we can learn lessons from the apolitical
nature of everyday life, which functions smoothly in
spite of the things that divide us. "In our civil society,
we naturally come together with people who are quite
different from us politically, racially, religiously, to do
cooperative things," he said. "When's the last time you
heard about doctors in a hospital refusing to perform a
heart surgery because they voted differently or because
they were a different race? So the fiber of American life
in a civic sense promotes cooperation. I think this is a
big, big deal."

Building bridges between people from different walks
of life demands a different perspective on the same circumstances that cause others to feel divided. It requires
a commitment to the development of authentic relationships, the use of dynamic communication techniques,
and a realization that service opportunities break down
social, cultural, and political barriers. It calls for a recognition that an attitude of inclusion is a hallmark of
successful bridge building – and that exclusion, insults,
and shame corrode the paths to social justice.

"The people who have made the most social change
have been the ones who tell an inspiring story that
draws a larger circle, that draws people in," Patel said.
"Building a diverse democracy is about three things. It's
really about engaging with the deep problem of marginalization, it's about bridging polarization, and it's
about being able to handle deep disagreements." Some
of those disagreements are "rooted in deep and fundamental identities," he said. And those identities must be
honored, reimagined, or even confronted, depending on
the circumstances.

Latasha Morrison is doing just that. In 2015, Morrison founded Be the Bridge, a nonprofit devoted to pursuing racial reconciliation through small groups, education, and spiritual talks. As a Christian minister and an African American, she works from within the church to foster connections. She travels throughout the country speaking to churches – in many cases majority-White, evangelical congregations – about the need for her fellow Christians to confront the racism, biases, and insensitivities that they have wielded for centuries against people of color, especially Black people. Morrison wrote a powerful book, *Be the Bridge*, on the same topic in 2019 and runs a Facebook group of the same name, using her platform to call Americans into robust conversations about racism and into relationships with people who aren't like them.[27]

When Morrison talks about our nation's history of systemic racism – and how White Christians, in particular, have fueled social injustice – she is showing them how someone who reads the same Bible and prays to the same God has been afflicted by White privilege and White supremacy. What she asks of them is to "lament" the past, to learn about it, and to apply lessons from it to their lives. "The type of bridge we're building is one that uplifts marginalized voices," she said. "We're truth-tellers – that's one of our values."

As a result, Morrison chooses to engage with people of difference who haven't yet figured it out. They can be rough around the edges, but if they've signaled a willingness to engage, she's in. "We give each other grace because there's going to be times when I need grace," she said. "Sometimes people are going to need grace to be ignorant and to ask a stupid question. I feel like no one gets this by yelling or demeaning them. So I think it's important that we do this with grace, we do this with love and truth. We want to see justice."

Morrison draws a careful distinction between

lamenting and shaming – "to me, lament elevates God," while "shame elevates you" – but she is also careful to note that it's still important to stand up to people who exude exclusion and ignorance, even when it makes them shift in their seats. Having difficult conversations about racism often causes White people to react defensively, as author Robin DiAngelo noted in her 2018 book, *White Fragility*. Which is why White people, in particular, need to cast aside their discomfort with conversations about their own racism.

"Am I doing something to tear you down? Or am I just saying some things that make you uncomfortable?" Morrison asked. "There's a difference. Am I attacking you as an individual, or am I telling the truth about a system of brokenness that we've ingested? It just really takes some discernment, and we can't go off of feelings. Sometimes we need time to process this." Calling people out for the sake of embarrassing them is often counterproductive, she said, because it's "about demeaning and not bringing solutions." It often brings about the opposite reaction that is desired. Yet it's critical to ensure that people aren't being silenced for the sake of creating an edifice of civility, which simply triggers identity corrosion underneath the surface. "It causes trauma when we isolate and oppress people, when they can't use their voice," Morrison said. "For centuries here in this country, that has happened where, if you spoke out or complained or if you called out, you would die. . . . I want to challenge people to have a different perspective, to learn from someone's different experience."

When I spoke with Morrison, she had just recently returned from speaking to a White evangelical church in Longview, Texas, a town on the eastern side of the state that political observers might label as blood-red for its conservative credentials. In Gregg County, where Longview is located, 69 percent of voters supported Donald Trump for president in 2016, while only 28 percent voted for Hillary Clinton.[28] "I went in there, and I spoke some hard truth, but this was not rocky ground. This soil was ready for this message," she said. "It may have been uncomfortable for some people, but they were ready to recognize some truth. If that's happening in east Texas, that's happening in other places."

—⚓—

This book is not about literal bridge builders – as in the architects, engineers, and contractors who design and construct physical structures to bring two sides together. But their real-life processes provide lessons for metaphorical bridge building.

Using the "segmental" process, crews build small sections at a time as the span gradually widens across the ground below. In metaphorical bridge building, progress is often incremental and organic and hard-won – but the sum adds up to revolutionary change in the long run. Braver Angels is taking this approach by helping Americans gradually stitch back together the bonds of social trust.[29]

Using the "cantilever" process, the span takes shape from the top of pre-built support pillars, gradually extending outward until each section attaches to the next section and ultimately forms a bridge connecting both sides of the gap. In metaphorical bridge building, people span gaps by leveraging existing connections or forming brand new relationships and then building outward from there. Eboo Patel is taking this approach with IFYC, as he seeks to empower members of different religious groups to extend toward each other.

Using the "incremental launching" process, a bridge deck is pre-assembled off-site and then pushed from one side of the gap to the other side. In other words, the bridge does not get constructed from both sides and reach completion by meeting in the middle. Similarly, in metaphorical bridge building, one common misconception is

that people must always meet in the middle. That's not
the case. What we see in the metaphorical process is that
sometimes bridges must be built from one side of the
gap to the other. This is what Latasha Morrison is promoting as she guides White Christians to abandon their
old ways of inaction and complacency and build bridges
toward Black Americans whom they've oppressed for
centuries.

Finally, in the rehabilitation process, crews recon-
struct or restore existing bridges that have become
dilapidated. Much like in real-life renovation, metaphorical bridge building often involves the renewal of
decrepit bridges that have become difficult or impossible
to traverse.

No matter the method, bridge builders must first
measure the length of the proposed span before deciding how to proceed. At the same time, they must assess
the nature of the soil that will ultimately support the
bridge's foundation. Then they must construct a firm
foundation from which to erect the bridge. Lacking an
adequate foundation, bridges can sink into the ground
and become unusable, defeating the ultimate purpose,
which is to facilitate exchanges between current and
future generations. There's always a risk that the bridge
will fail if it's not properly designed. A bridge collapse
is, of course, devastating from a human, economic, and
political perspective, which simply underscores the need
to get it right in the first place.

Likewise, metaphorical bridge builders need to assess
the status of the social, political, and cultural situations
they face before proceeding with their projects. They
must understand history, honor it, and learn from it to
ensure they're constructing a bridge that will last.

"The type of bridge you're going to build . . . has to
be a function of where you're building it," said Pinar
Okumus, a structural engineering professor and member
of the board at the University at Buffalo's Institute for

Bridge Engineering. "For example, steel bridges tend to be lighter than concrete bridges, so if you try to build a heavy concrete bridge on a soil that cannot support it, then your foundation would be terribly expensive."

History is full of examples of bridges revolutionizing society:

- The Brooklyn Bridge's opening in 1883 marked the first span between Manhattan and Brooklyn, greatly improving transportation and paving the way for them to merge five years later.[30]
- The Ponte Vecchio in Florence, Italy, was initially built sometime before 966 and reconstructed after a flood in 1345. It became a vital connecting route for the region, provided a place for locals to sell goods in shops overlooking the river Arno, and survived World War II as an "everlasting symbol" of hope for the city.[31]
- The Nanjing Yangtze River Bridge, built in China in 1968 during dictator Mao Zedong's oppressive Cultural Revolution, enabled easy transportation for people who previously had to cross by ferry and for trains that previously had to be disassembled and loaded onto boats to make their way across.[32]

There are countless others. The point is that bridges enable dynamic change. They breed engagement. But building them requires sophisticated design, engineering, material sourcing, and plain old-fashioned hard work. "Sometimes when people hear the term 'bridge building' ... they don't think it's going to be hard, they don't think they're going to be uncomfortable, they don't think they're going to be challenged," Morrison said. "It's going to be difficult. It's going to be uncomfortable."

To be clear, this book will not commit the sin of false equivalence – that is, the tendency to give equal weight

to two sides that do not deserve equivalent considera-
tion. As such, I will not suggest that everyone needs to
meet squarely in the middle. That's because in some
cases, one side is right and the other side is wrong, plain
and simple. Moreover, I don't want to suggest that
bridge building solves all our problems. It simply sets
the stage for us to achieve progress through new policies, for example.

Rather, this book serves as a forensic dissection of the
bridge building strategies employed by leaders who are
going against the polarized grain. It seeks to illuminate
the ways in which people are overcoming gaping divides
in areas such as politics, race, religion, class, and culture
– and how we can apply those lessons to our lives and to
the institutions that govern society.

And I say "overcoming" because bridge building is
a journey that's never truly complete. It's a process – a
lifestyle, if you will. After all, bridges need maintenance
almost as soon as they are constructed. They get potholes. They rust. And they become obsolete if we neglect
them.

As I considered whom to feature, I decided not to
write about anyone particularly famous. That way you
won't have preexisting opinions about them. I also
thought it was critical to feature a diversity of voices
because we can't learn how to build bridges effectively
without listening to experienced people from a broad
cross-section of backgrounds who have approached the
process from many different angles. Similarly, I decided
to feature people from a wide range of sectors, including
government, faith, nonprofit, business, education, and
journalism. Each person's expertise is vital, just as the
builders of physical bridges have a wide variety of experiences in areas ranging from environmental assessment
to material science to structural integrity.

"Everyone within that system is important, and it's
important that they communicate with each other and

bridge that knowledge gap that exists between them in a very seamless manner," said Atorod Azizinamini, a renowned bridge engineer who chairs Florida International University's Department of Civil and Environmental Engineering. "If one area fails, it can cause the complete collapse of the bridge."

Despite its transformational qualities, bridge building often attracts considerable resistance – sometimes legitimate, sometimes not so much – from environmental activists, budget hawks, developers, and locals with not-in-my-backyard (NIMBY) syndrome. In many cases, that's because bridges promise to disrupt the status quo for people who previously benefited from or preferred social isolation.

But new bridges are often necessary despite the risks and despite the opposition they engender. They're the only way to reach the other side. After all, nobody changes the world from the isolation of an island.

Exceptional bridges transcend the basic functionality and economic vitality they were designed to provide. People take trips to see great bridges. They walk across them, take pictures of them, and depict them in artwork. Great bridges capture our imagination. They are feats of engineering. "That's why there are so many beautiful designs out there," said Azizinamini, who was honored by the White House in 2015 for making the nation's bridges safer.[33] "People identify a location, a community, a city by that bridge."

When we build bridges, entire societies are often transformed.

"If I tell you, 'San Francisco,'" Azizinamini said, "what's the first thing that comes to your mind?"

Part I

Forging a Path toward Reconciliation

We still live in a racially segregated society. We are separate and unequal.

Our schools, our friendships, our religious services, our neighborhoods, our cities, our civic gatherings – all these environments remain largely divided by race. The demise of Jim Crow laws may have technically outlawed the segregation of physical facilities, such as bathrooms, buses, schools, restaurants, and hospitals, but we are far from being an integrated society. So it should come as no surprise that so many White people like myself remain blind to racial injustices. We remain blind to the oppression of Black people in many areas of life, such as education, jobs, healthcare, and criminal justice. We remain blind to the plight of immigrants living in America without documentation, to the plight of people seeking to keep their families together when they cross the Mexican border, and to the plight of refugees who are seeking a future in what we once called the Land of Opportunity. And in many cases, of course, we are not blind at all – we are directly perpetuating racial injustice and continued segregation, whether we realize it or not.

Why are we so unwilling to grapple with the challenges our fellow humans face? Because they aren't our neighbors. Because they aren't our fellow congregants. Because they aren't our classmates. Just about the only place where Americans regularly interact with people of another race or ethnicity is in the workplace, where they usually have no choice. When given an option, most White Americans choose to stay ensconced in their comfortable social bubbles.

Fewer than half of Americans frequently interact with friends of other races or ethnicities, while only a quarter frequently interact with people of other races or ethnicities at religious services, according to a 2019 study by the *Atlantic* and the Public Religion Research Institute. Fewer than one in five Americans say they frequently do so at local civic gatherings, such as club events or school meetings. And about one in five seldom or never interact with someone of another race or ethnicity in any setting.[1] Let that sink in.

In other words, as White people, we don't need Jim Crow to keep segregation intact. We're taking care of that on our own – and it's shameful.

To be clear, people of color do not bear responsibility for this massive gulf. They have been subject to centuries of injustice at the hands of White oppressors. They should not be expected to build bridges to the other side, even though they frequently do so. Rather, White people need to step up and begin a journey of introspection, memorialization, lamentation, and reconciliation that must occur to demolish the barriers that continue to separate us from people who are Black, Indigenous, and other people of color, including immigrants.

A lack of meaningful relationships between people of difference is one of, if not the most, significant drivers of our continued division in America. It prevents us from engaging in conversation, which would breed more understanding and a greater willingness to call for policy change to address lingering problems. It blocks our kids from forming friendships with people who don't look like them. It encourages White people to perpetuate our White privilege, driving the systemic racism that continuously gets us ahead. A lack of meaningful relationships partly explains why, for example, White people continue to deny that Black people are often actively prevented from achieving the same economic, social, and political progress as White people. It also leads many White people to embrace the misinformation and misdirection of political leaders who actively deny, misconstrue, or outright lie about the role of racism in America today. Only about one-quarter of White Americans agreed in 2019 that "slavery has a great deal of an effect" on the status of Black people today, while about six in ten Black people said it does, according to the Pew Research Center.[2] We should not be shocked that many Americans deny the legacy of slavery. If seeing is believing, then White people will remain culturally and politically ignorant until we establish the types of relationships that will prompt us to open our eyes.

Coupled with our human tendency to prize group loyalty over the pursuit of truth – a tendency well documented by Yale's Cultural Cognition Project – we fail to absorb what other people are saying, in part because they're so far away. Intolerance, racism, and inequality continue to fester.

Yes, policy change is necessary to achieve tangible progress on key issues caused by systemic racism, like a lack of access to good schools, economic inequality, and unaffordable medical care. That is the ultimate goal. But until White people begin to authentically see Black Americans as family, friends, and neighbors, we won't accept the premise that anything needs to change. Our hearts will remain hardened, and segregation will endure – because people in power will see no need to shake things up when their constituents aren't pressing for change.

The encouraging news is that, in 2020, many Americans began to open their eyes to the endemic racism that continues to plague our country. In the wake of the highly public killings of Ahmaud Arbery, Breonna Taylor, and George Floyd in rapid succession, certain White people began contemplating, for the first time, the premise that their indifference – or, in many cases, their actions – has played and continues to play a central role in harming and undermining people of color. In 2016, just over a quarter of Americans approved of the Black Lives Matter movement. Four years later, in the aftermath of Floyd's killing at the hands of the Minneapolis police and the uprising that occurred on the streets of American cities following his death, support for Black Lives Matter soared to 57 percent.[3]

That surge in support reflected a marked shift in public opinion that paves the way for sweeping cultural change – but only if we embrace the techniques of bridge builders in cultivating relationships and conversation between people of difference.

In this part, I'll tell the stories of people who are refusing to settle for the dysfunctional status quo defined by racial, ethnic, and cultural barriers. They believe that we can forge a path toward reconciliation by immersing ourselves in community. And that's what they're doing.

They believe that simply being present is the first step in bringing people together. They believe in the power of lasting, authentic personal connections to foster transformation. But they don't run from interpersonal conflict. They embrace it within the context of a collective mindset. And they believe that the people who build the longest-lasting bridges are the ones willing to challenge their contemporaries to join them on a journey toward truth.

1

From Blindness to Sight

Jane Carrigan took a slow sip of her drink at a coffee shop in Annapolis, Maryland, set her cup down, and extended her arm toward me across a small rectangular table. She rolled up her sleeve, her hand clenched tightly in a fist, so I could see her forearm. "I think I embody both," she said, pointing at her lightly toned Black skin. "The enslaved and the enslaver. And it means something."

Growing up, Carrigan knew that her family traced its lineage back to Cape Verde, which was a colony of Portugal until it declared its independence in 1975. "My maiden name was Spencer. Spencer is a very well-known name in Cape Verde," said Carrigan, a retiree from the National Institutes of Health.

When her ancestors were still living there, the transatlantic trade of enslaved people was booming from the volcanic archipelago about 350 miles west of modern-day Senegal. "They were very important during the slave trade. This I did not know until I was a grown woman," Carrigan said. "The slavers would go to the Slave Coast and capture their slaves, and then they would take them to Cape Verde and keep them there, go back to the Slave Coast, collect some more, bring them back to Cape Verde, and hold them until the winds were right to go across the Atlantic."

What Carrigan eventually discovered is that her ancestral heritage is inextricably intertwined with Cape Verde's history as a launching pad for centuries of injustice. A pair of Spencers, she found out, were her ancestors: they were brothers, and they were White. One eventually wound up in the Windward Islands, while the other one settled in the Leeward Islands – both on the eastern edge of the Caribbean Sea.

"Well, it turns out they were slavers," Carrigan said. In all likelihood, she believes, based on her research of her genealogy, they likely raped the Black women they had enslaved, impregnating them. "So I come from slavers," she said.

Carrigan's desire to explore her own identity eventually brought her to a meeting of the group Coming to the Table, which promotes racial healing while confronting the legacy of slavery in a variety of settings, including businesses, churches, and schools. Formed in 2009, Coming to the Table has grown into a national organization that holds gatherings designed to promote conversation, transformational personal relationships, and restorative justice.

Echoing the Rev. Martin Luther King, Jr.'s hope, articulated in his "I Have a Dream" speech that "one day . . . the sons of former slaves and the sons of former slave owners will be able to sit down together at the table of brotherhood,"[1] Coming to the Table's board has historically endeavored to have a roughly equal mix of members descended from people who were enslaved and members descended from those who "held, owned, or traded" people.[2]

"I kept coming back because it felt right," Carrigan said. "And I began to talk about my story – realizing that my story isn't the typical Black American story, but that doesn't matter, really, with Coming to the Table."

After becoming a faithful participant in the group's meetings, Carrigan became the lead facilitator of the

Annapolis chapter, secretary of the national organization, and a champion for the group's devotion to conversation as a catalyst for change. "What we do at Coming to the Table – what we hope to do at least – is we provide a safe space for that kind of conversation to happen among all people," she said.

What 2020 surely showed us is that, for this country to begin addressing systemic racism, we must embrace the type of dynamic relationships and conversation that Coming to the Table promotes. Without the interpersonal form of restorative justice that Coming to the Table cultivates, we cannot begin building a bridge from our history of racial injustice to a future of racial equity and equality.

"We talk about being an organization of the descendants of the enslaved and the descendants of enslavers," Carrigan said, "but really we are an organization that is about privilege and White privilege and racism and how that affects people – positively and negatively, and sometimes in ways they don't even realize."

<hr />

Tom DeWolf, who is White, was once among those who didn't realize how much White privilege and racism had affected his life. In the 1980s, when DeWolf owned a restaurant in Bend, Oregon, a chance encounter with a distant relative led to a family trip to Cape Cod to explore his personal history. That's when he discovered that he is related to Herman Melville, the famous author of *Moby Dick*, who had married into the family.

Sure enough, in Chapter 45 of *Moby Dick*, Melville names a character Captain D'Wolf[3] – "because the DeWolfs were big seafaring captains," Tom said. Indeed, as he continued to investigate his roots, DeWolf soon learned that his lineage included slave traders, rum runners, and privateers. He remembers experiencing a feeling of emotional detachment when he found out. It hadn't yet sunk in. "I didn't really get a sense of it all," he said.

About a decade and a half later, however, DeWolf received an invitation to join a group of distant cousins on a trip to further explore their family history. That's when he discovered the full scope of his ancestry. The DeWolfs, it turns out, were "the largest slave-trading dynasty in US history," he said. "They were responsible for something like 100 or 105 voyages that would travel from Rhode Island to west Africa and trade rum or whatever for African people – and then brought them to 30 or 40 different ports in North and South America and the Caribbean."

That life-changing experience nudged DeWolf to further confront his family roots, which were woven into America's thick fabric of racial injustice and inequity. That journey of personal reckoning led him to join a gathering in 2006 at the Center for Justice and Peacebuilding (CJP) at Eastern Mennonite University (EMU) in Harrisonburg, Virginia, to begin discussing the formation of the group that later became Coming to the Table. The people who organized the gathering included descendants of the Hairston family, which includes thousands of people descended from enslavers as well as people descended from those who were enslaved. The meeting also included descendants of former US President Thomas Jefferson and his wife, Martha, as well as descendants of Jefferson and a woman he enslaved, Sally Hemings. "That's where Coming to the Table got started," DeWolf said.

The group took a few years to get grant funding and launch officially, eventually launching in partnership with CJP, which laid the groundwork for the foundation of principles defining Coming to the Table, including the importance of trauma awareness, restorative justice, and conflict resolution. From the beginning, the group's mission was rooted in a core belief that

community building happens through intentional conversation and the cultivation of relationships between
people of difference.

"The focus is on an invitation to change the hearts and
minds of individuals. Because until we do that, changing
the laws doesn't change the fundamental issues around
White supremacy and a legacy of slavery," said DeWolf,
who still leads the national group, now affiliated with
Restorative Justice for Oakland Youth, as program
manager. "So this is a focus on building relationships,
understanding, acknowledging all the history, working
toward healing, and taking action to undo the systems
and structures that keep people separated and keep
White people on top in an unfair system."

On Martin Luther King, Jr. Day in January 2019, I
strolled up a redbrick walkway along the tree-shrouded
entrance of the Unitarian Universalist Church of
Annapolis. The rustic wooden structure funneled to
an obtuse triangle overhanging the doorway, steps
away from a Black Lives Matter sign displayed on the
church's lawn.

At DeWolf's invitation, I had come to this meeting
place for the monthly gathering of the Annapolis session
of Coming to the Table, led by Carrigan. When I got
there, the group was still arranging about a dozen chairs
in a circle near the stage. Several participants greeted
me, and Carrigan informed the group of my presence
as an author. I told them about my project and that I
was honored to participate in the session, but would not
reveal anything said there, in a spirit of maintaining the
group's commitment to confidentiality. Then the group
started with the distribution of a handout.

On one side was a brief summary of Coming to
the Table's mission and values, including "inclusion,"
"respect and tolerance," "justice," "compassion, mercy,

and forgiveness," "peace and nonviolence," "love," and "honesty, truthfulness, and transparency." These values immediately struck me as antithetical to our fiercely polarized political culture, which is characterized by intolerance, bitterness, gracelessness, and hate.

On the other side of the handout was a list of six guidelines for sharing during a discussion rooted in reconciliation:

1. We will practice deep listening and staying totally present with the person speaking.
2. We will practice mindful speech.
3. We will avoid giving advice.
4. We will be mindful of our participation level.
5. Whenever possible, we will acknowledge uncomfortable responses: say 'ouch!' or 'oops!' then explain.
6. All that arises here is confidential.

The guidelines for this circle discussion process further explained that interrupting each other was not allowed. Each person was supposed to pause after the previous speaker finished talking to give the speaker's comments time to sink in. And participants were encouraged to share with others if the comments felt hurtful and to help the group understand the reasons for their reactions.

As a matter of principle, each person spoke only when the predetermined "talking piece" was handed to them – in our case, some sort of red rubber paperweight. Before beginning the discussion, we went around the circle one by one, with each of us taking turns to read a few sentences of the guidelines out loud to make sure everyone had absorbed them.

Those guidelines naturally came with a degree of discomfort. This was nothing like the workplace, where we can share our thoughts with our colleagues through instant messages, emails, or conversations. It was nothing like home, where we can instantly spout off to our family members about the news of the day. And it was certainly nothing like social media, where we can blast our hot takes to the world – where opinions are plentiful, loudness is rewarded, and sensationalism is currency.

To spur topical conversation, Carrigan handed out an article on MLK Day, and we took turns in reading a few lines out loud. When we had finished reading the story, we went around the circle and shared our perspectives one by one. By virtue of our seating positions, several people had the talking piece before me. When my turn came, I strained to pause following the previous person's remarks to let her thoughts sink in, as I had seen others do. It felt like forever, even though it was really only a few seconds. I wasn't used to this.

And then I spoke. I shared my thoughts. They felt inconsequential to me. And they probably were. As a White man, why should anyone listen to my thoughts about the legacy of racism? White people have been responsible for centuries of racial injustice against Black people – and we continue to benefit from that legacy in ways both seen and unseen. Yet as I made eye contact with the other members of the group, including White people and Black people, I could feel that they were still listening. Genuinely listening. They were trying to absorb what I had to say.

After I spoke, I realized that the guidelines weren't really about ensuring that people listened to me. Rather, they were about ensuring that I spoke thoughtfully, not hurtfully or carelessly. Without thinking about it, I had adopted the slow, deliberate cadence of the others in the circle. As we conversed, this unusual form of discourse had the natural effect of encouraging us to deeply ponder each other's thoughts and feelings.

"We provide a safe space for that kind of conversation to happen," Carrigan told me in our interview.

"We're very careful to say there's no judgment. There is no cross-talk. We don't try to fix anybody because nobody's broken. And we allow the conversation to happen."

That doesn't mean that participants can't confront insensitive or racist comments or perspectives. Quite the opposite. "We talk about calling people – not calling them out, but calling them in," Carrigan said. As in, "let me call you in on your stuff and tell you why that sounded wrong or sounded hurtful to me."

But expressing your perspectives is only a small part of Coming to the Table. Most of it is listening. "It's really deep listening," Carrigan said. "Because you might say something that I react to, but I've got six people to listen to before I get to react to what you said. And that does change how I ultimately answer."

Bridge builders recognize that active listening has a greater healing effect than talking. It forces us to consider what life must be like from the other person's vantage point. And that creates a special bond of empathy that breaks down interpersonal barriers.

This is not just wishful thinking. Empirical research on the circle discussion process has concluded that it "can make the attitudes of the parties involved more balanced and less extreme and thus increasing the chances of resolving the conflict."[4]

Active listening, whether from the perimeter of a circle or in another context, doesn't just help you understand the other person. It helps you understand yourself. It forces you to take a step back and seriously consider your own perspectives before proceeding with your commentary. It teaches you to be slow to speak, which stands in stark contrast to a culture that teaches us that speaking is the best way to begin taking action.

"This is expanding the understanding of what action is – that you and I having this conversation is a form of action if it's leading to new understanding or expanded awareness," DeWolf said. "And the building of relationships – authentic, accountable relationships – allows for the opportunity to see life as experienced from someone different than myself that I wouldn't otherwise ever experience or understand."

Several weeks after attending the Coming to the Table session in Annapolis, I spoke with Jodie Geddes. Geddes, who was born in Jamaica and grew up in Brooklyn, serves as a community organizer at Restorative Justice for Oakland Youth. While earning her master's degree in conflict transformation from EMU's Center for Justice and Peacebuilding several years ago, Geddes went to a session of Coming to the Table for the first time.

"For me as a Black woman in a space that primarily had White folks in that first meeting, I felt really blocked emotionally from being empathetic when others were sharing their stories," she said. "And I think the challenge of that space was the reason that I continued to attend Coming to the Table meetings because I wanted to explore what that was."

As she continued attending, she came to "explore my own reflections on my relationship with White people beyond their Whiteness," she said. After becoming more involved in Coming to the Table, she was eventually appointed as president of the organization's advisory board. Restorative justice, she said, is the primary goal of the conversations taking place at Coming to the Table sessions throughout the country.

"Restorative justice [doesn't] give priority to one voice over another," she said. "It's really about the examination of privilege, of things like equity and things like power. The circle process allows someone, when they have the talking piece, to share their truth in whatever way that is for them. But it allows for the rest of the circle to be witnesses to the truth of that person."

The pursuit of restorative justice through the circle process has deep roots. It "comes from Indigenous and Afrocentric traditions of community – community building, community organizing – that's really about honoring the dignity of every single person," she said. "'Restorative justice' says, 'How do we have a healing justice instead of a harming justice?'" While it's often described as "a process to deal with what people call crime or harm," Geddes views it as "a practice of remembering" – that is, "remembering how to be in deep community and relationship with each other, so that when harm and conflict emerge, we can lean into that in healthy ways and still maintain relationships as we work through conflict."

Conflict is not only natural in the process of bridge building – it's inevitable. But the key to ensuring that the bridge comes together is to emphasize that differences in culture, class, and personality between people on either side should be cherished, not diminished or attacked. Appreciating those basic human differences is critical to addressing conflicting perspectives.

Society often views "people as disposable," Geddes said. "The beautiful thing about restorative justice is it says, 'Lean into the conflict.' We can still have conflict but leave the conversation as friends. So it's shifting our lens." The lens can be shifted by focusing on the facts, including the lessons of history that are often excluded from school textbooks and ignored in conversations about current events. That requires acknowledging the culture of violence that has been wielded to persecute and subjugate people of color for centuries.

"It's recognizing the damage, memorializing it, understanding it, honoring it, working on all the ways that we can build resilience and build relationships, build confidence, and build health," DeWolf said. "We've got tools in place to help people manage conflict in ways that we're not often taught to do. We normally fight, flee, or freeze. It's not often that we approach things from a real rational basis because our instinct is to do those other things."

For many people, there's a natural trepidation about discussing the legacy of slavery and related issues, which often manifests itself at Coming to the Table gatherings. "I think we all want to be seen, but we're afraid to be witnessed," Geddes said. "If we ask people to show us the deepest parts of themselves, are we . . . ready to be vulnerable with them? Sometimes in society we ask people to do things that we're not willing to do ourselves. And we need a space to explore what that means, but we also need a space to explore something that is different."

Coming to the Table organizers acknowledge that the people who participate in their gatherings are naturally inclined to bridge racial divides. But what about people who don't want to talk about it or who deny that it's an issue altogether? I asked DeWolf about this.

"I recognize that there are people who just flat out don't want to deal with racism," he said. "If people are willing to get into a conversation about this, if people are reaching out to Coming to the Table, more than likely they are interested to some degree in finding out what's going on with themselves, or in their community, in their family." But he said one of the group's goals is to help White people understand the need for them to learn more about the legacy of slavery, racism, and White privilege. As more do so, the hope is that they will begin to change others around them. "Until we do, we perpetuate the inequality and the injustice, and we pass it onto our kids," DeWolf said. "So that's our choice. Either I, as a White person, deal with this stuff and work toward healing and transformation, or I am in fact perpetuating racism and injustice."

In many cases, it's political conservatives who are most resistant to change on these issues. They bear a significant share of the responsibility in bridging these divides. But conservatives aren't the only ones capable of perpetuating racism and injustice – and thus they aren't the only ones who need to deal with these issues. Some liberals think they should be exempt from this process of examining and addressing the legacy of injustice because of their supposedly progressive beliefs on race – but they shouldn't be exempt, DeWolf said. They may even devote personal time to consuming information about America's history of racism, but if they're not immersing themselves in relationships and conversations with people of color, it's difficult for them to form authentic interpersonal connections and thus difficult for them to truly understand the depths of these issues.

"There are many White people that I've met over the years who will do the reading and they'll watch the documentaries, but they don't engage on a daily basis with people of color or people of difference," Geddes said. "So folks need to challenge themselves to go outside of their communities."

In the years after its initial meeting, Coming to the Table enjoyed a modicum of success in establishing groups throughout the country and gaining attention for its nontraditional approach to tackling the legacy of slavery. By Election Day 2016, the organization had about 10 affiliate groups, 1,500 members in its private Facebook group, and 500 subscribers to its newsletter.

But Donald Trump's election brought the nation's cultural divides into sharper focus. For many, his ascent empowered their racism. For others, however, it sparked a desire to pursue reconciliation.

In the aftermath of the election, interest in Coming to the Table surged. By early May 2020, the organization had more than 40 affiliate groups, about 4,700 members in its Facebook group, and thousands of subscribers to its newsletter. Weeks later, interest surged anew amid a national outpouring of grief and rage stemming from rising awareness of police violence against Black people and the systemic racial injustice that continues to seize our communities. On May 25, video of White Minneapolis police officer Derek Chauvin killing George Floyd circulated widely on social media. The devastating footage spurred outrage in Minneapolis and in cities throughout America.[5]

It was the latest in a long string of high-profile police killings of Black people. But many have gone largely unnoticed by social media and the press. From 2015 through 2020, police shot and killed more than 5,000 people throughout America, according to a *Washington Post* database.[6] Police killings of Black Americans have included many who were unarmed, such as Michael Brown in Ferguson, Missouri, in 2014,[7] Antwon Rose II in Pittsburgh in 2018,[8] and Breonna Taylor in Louisville in 2020.[9] From 2010 through 2020, at least 32 people died after saying they couldn't breathe due to fatal police holds – and three-fourths of those victims were Black men, many of whom had been stopped for minor infractions, according to a *USA Today* analysis.[10]

While protests and unrest followed some of those killings, the national uprising after Floyd's death reached new heights. Countless protesters hit the streets throughout the country to voice their anger about police brutality against Black people and general racial injustice.

The discontent did not just stay on the streets. It swept through corporate America, professional sports, legislative chambers, city councils, police departments, schools, families, and community organizations. The collective response drew more White people into the national conversation about racism than the leaders of Coming to the Table had ever seen before.

way, the uproar marked the first time many people finally began listening to the cries of Black , who had never stopped grappling with systemic racism despite the downfall of slavery and Jim Crow. For many White people, the tension that enveloped the nation made them uncomfortable. But being uncomfortable is often the only way for bridges to be built. No bridge can rise without first disrupting the property where the span will be built. Sometimes, demolition is necessary before construction can begin. It's going to look messy for a while.

That mess simply means that construction is under way. Yet we can't begin to repair brokenness until we fully understand what is broken. It's tantamount to the concept of trauma awareness, which is central to the identity of Coming to the Table.

It's about "understanding what trauma is, what it does, how it gets perpetuated, how it gets passed on generationally," DeWolf said when I reconnected with him after the movement for racial justice took off. "Breaking free of those cycles of violence is the key to healing. And there's a healing journey that takes place."

There is often a temptation for those of us who are White to try to fix things immediately. But events like the death of George Floyd show us that we can't begin to fix anything until we authentically engage with the deep roots of the problem. We need to properly acknowledge and lament the painful path of Black people through the harmful structures of racism and oppression that we, as White people, have sustained, whether purposely or indirectly.

Yes, we can and should pursue reconciliation. But we must recognize that the pursuit sometimes requires us to be still at first so that we can truly understand the need to embrace motion. Otherwise the pursuit often stems from selfish motivations.

"There's a lot of White folks that come to this work

and they just want to go right to reconciliation without doing all of the other critical work of repair, of acknowledgment, of memorialization, of apology, of confronting the offender when the offender is society or your mom, and jump right to the end game, which is, 'How can I feel better as quickly as possible and get rid of these feelings of shame and guilt?'" DeWolf said.

For centuries, White people like me have had the privilege of ignoring the structural issues stemming from racism that have affected Black people in innumerable ways, ranging from criminal injustice to insufficient schools to a lack of voting rights to unequal access to healthcare to real estate discrimination. Now, these challenges are harder to ignore than ever. That's good. But they *can* still be ignored, which is why it's critical to begin creating an avenue for conversations about their roots in places where silence would otherwise prevail.

The Coming to the Table model offers a pathway to creating such a space where relationships can be built between people of difference and where people can begin to more deeply internalize the wide-ranging legacy of slavery and systemic racism. "If we're going to change the world, transform our world into a place free of racism and bias and prejudice and inequality and oppression in all of its expressions, we need to transform individuals one heart at a time and get to this tipping point where the way we've been for centuries, for millennia, is no longer acceptable," DeWolf said.

To be sure, many White Americans reflexively decried the civil unrest that occurred in the wake of George Floyd's killing. They trashed the peaceful protestors by pointing out isolated instances of looting, for example, and other incidents of violence, while refusing to acknowledge the numerous examples of police brutality against the protestors. The reality is that the protests reflected a concrete example of many Black and White people coming together to vocalize their unwillingness

to wait any longer for systemic change. And that movement was a transformational form of bridge building – a
collective relationship of sorts between people on the
ground – that marked a serious turning point toward
racial justice and equity for Black Americans.

"This is such a pivotal, even energetic, spiritual
moment in our world," Geddes told me when we reconnected. "Even White folks that want to can't escape it."
I asked both DeWolf and Geddes whether they would
describe what we witnessed in the aftermath of Floyd's
death as an awakening of sorts. They both said no – it's
more than that.

"A more apt analogy in my mind is that we've been
blind," DeWolf said, speaking of White people. "It's
like a horse with blinders on, so they can only see in
front of them. There's all this stuff still on both sides
of them – they just can't see it because of the blinders.
Taking those off so we can see the full spectrum of our
world – that's what it feels like to me."

Going from blindness to sight doesn't necessarily
guarantee that change will occur, however. You can see
injustice and do nothing about it. You can read about
it and do nothing, too. What's necessary is for White
people to forge authentic relationships and engage in
conversations with Black people and other people of
color – and then to begin using their platforms to help
empower their colleagues and bring about change.

"Now there is no excuse for White silence. They have
to take action," Geddes said. "We don't have any more
bandages to cover all of the scars, all of the scabs, all of
the wounds. There's been this one dirty bandage that
we've been using to wrap everything in, and it doesn't
stick anymore."

———

Outside groups have begun to take notice of Coming
to the Table's approach. In early 2019, for example,

the school district in Anne Arundel County, which includes Annapolis, invited Jane Carrigan to explain how teachers and administrators could use Coming to the Table's model to begin a discussion about race in their schools.[11] The invitation came after a series of racist incidents stirred tension, including "a petition circulated at Arundel High School by the 'Kool Kids Klan'" and "a noose hung at Crofton Middle School," according to the *Capital Gazette*.[12]

Coming to the Table's model of restorative justice coupled with trauma awareness provides a route for institutions like the Anne Arundel schools to begin rectifying the bitter conflicts that threaten to ensure further division. "As human beings, we tend to really beat the crap out of each other with enthusiasm, and we do a lot of shaming and blaming. We do a lot less of supporting each other in areas of repentance and apology and forgiveness and reparation," DeWolf said. "We have an opportunity all the time to do that, and we very rarely take it. The Coming to the Table approach would say, 'Let's do the hard work.'"

At times, our national conversation over race has been profoundly counterproductive – both before and after the death of George Floyd. According to one measurement, online hate speech reached an all-time high in early June 2020 at the peak of the street protests over racial justice.[13] But past progress encourages the leaders of Coming to the Table to believe that future progress is achievable. "There is no way that healing is not possible. I come from an ancestry and a lineage of Black bodies that saw what was possible and fought for the possibilities," Geddes said. "Someone dreamed of me, and I became possible. I must honor my ancestors. When I lose hope, I am not honoring them."

DeWolf said people's capacity for personal transformation is what gives him hope for a better tomorrow. It's "the recognition that we – each of us – have the power to transform," he said. "Our thoughts create our reality. Our attention, our focus goes to what we zoom into. So if I zoom into hope, that's where my attention goes."

To be sure, bridge building can be an achingly long process. Oftentimes it feels like construction goes on forever. The mess never stops being a mess, it seems. But the bridge advances, inch by inch, until, one day, people are walking across to the other side. "In native tradition, we talk about how we're building for the seventh generation forward and we're taking from the seventh generation backward," Geddes said. "What kind of mark am I leaving with my collective community for the generation to come? Everything does not have to happen in my time."

There's no denying that "it takes time," DeWolf said, but there's something transformative in the "commitment to spend the time and the energy to support each other in a journey that we've agreed to take together."

"That, to me, is the beauty of this approach when people commit to it," he said. "I love the name of this organization, and it's a great concept. But coming to the table honestly is pretty easy. It's staying at the table that matters."

2

From Human to Human

Years of war left vast swaths of Azar Maluki's country in ruins. Lives destroyed. Communities ripped apart. Infrastructure devastated. History lost. Spirits broken.

The US invasion of Iraq in 2003 was launched with the aim of regime change and the forcible installation of democracy under the false premise that dictator Saddam Hussein was harboring weapons of mass destruction. President George W. Bush pursued the conflict in the aftermath of 9/11, when the American thirst for revenge and hostility toward Islam and people living in the Middle East had reached a boiling point.

Despite the origins of the invasion, Maluki was glad to see the ruthless dictator ousted. Hussein, a Sunni Muslim, had presided over a reign of terror that afflicted the people of the holy Shia city of Najaf, where Maluki was born, grew up, and was living when American troops invaded in 2003. But when the war quickly devolved into a quagmire following Hussein's removal and execution, thrusting Iraq into a cyclone of violence and desperation, the Iraqi dermatologist watched helplessly as a shroud of despair enveloped his homeland.

"The war of 2003 was very much different from what we experienced in the past," Maluki said, gently clutching the handle of a white coffee cup emblazoned with the black outline of a dove. "It destroyed everything

47

– the buildings, the infrastructure. It destroyed the psychology of the Iraqi people." For Iraqis, "or most of them at least," he said, America came to be known as "war, the military uniforms walking the streets, the guns – machine guns."

An entire generation of Iraqi children grew up with American armed forces ever present. "Very young kids at that time, when they start seeing military uniforms – the Americans and other nations – they start raising their hands as a sign of surrender," he said. Maluki raised his arms and faced his palms outward, imitating the powerless Iraqi children he had seen countless times interacting with American troops. "They know that this person is dangerous. They threaten them," he said.

After years of death and destruction, Maluki was surrounded by brokenness. "Most Iraqis were hopeless," he said. "No light in the tunnel because everything's destroyed. It's years and years to rebuild everything." So when Maluki, his family, and a handful of other Iraqis greeted a small group of American civilian visitors to Najaf in 2012, he didn't know exactly what to expect. But he resolved not to make up his mind about them despite the devastation the war had brought upon his homeland. "You should never pre-judge people for their race or their name, skin color, nationality, religion," he said. "You should listen to them. You should talk to them."

Nonetheless, Maluki was surprised by what he saw next. He had never seen American civilians performing acts of service in Iraq – that is, not until the visitors from the other side of the world made their way to a section of road between Najaf and Karbala, about 100 miles from Baghdad.

The volunteers, part of the Minneapolis-based Iraqi and American Reconciliation Project (IARP), had come to the country to perform acts of service, form relationships, and conduct conversations with locals. Their overarching goal was to begin writing a new, positive chapter in the complicated story of Americans and Iraqis.

On the median of the newly constructed road, the Minnesotans planted tree saplings. It was particularly meaningful for the people of Najaf because of the ecological devastation that had occurred during the war, when the United States banned Iraqi planes from flying in the local airspace. "The date trees needed to be sprayed, and they weren't," said Kathy McKay, the founding executive director of IARP. "So a lot of them didn't produce dates, and a lot of them died."

Over the course of that November afternoon, the Americans planted about 75 trees with help from a local volunteer group as part of a broader beautification effort.[1] "It was a very slight offering back – a compensatory gift – since our planes blew everything up," McKay said.

The project, albeit small in scale, nonetheless had an outsized impact locally. It was such an unusual sight that an Iraqi news crew featured the volunteers in a TV broadcast. The report went something like this: "the Americans came to plant trees" instead of dropping bombs this time, McKay summarized.

For Maluki, the experience of seeing Americans without military uniforms do something good in his homeland resonated. "How could the American people behave like that?" he told me, encapsulating his thoughts at the time. "It was very important and very surprising also for Iraqis to have helping hands passing through from America."

His face transitioned slowly from a puzzled look into a grin. "The Iraqis started asking, 'Who are those Americans? Why are they doing this for us? Will they continue their work?'"

⁂

Born in Iraq, Sami Rasouli fled the country after Hussein's rise to power. "In the '80s, Saddam Hussein addressed the Iraqis, saying, 'If you're not with me, you're against me,'" Rasouli recalled. "Then I said, 'Wow, there is no room for me in Iraq to stay anymore.'"

Political liberty is essential to his being. "It's a matter of freedom," he said. "I have the right to choose what I should be, and Saddam Hussein had no right to force me to be one of his followers. So that's why I left Iraq."

He left for America, ultimately settling in Minneapolis, where he went on to own a combination grocery-store-bakery-restaurant focused on cuisine from his homeland. By the turn of the century, he had managed to build a comfortable life for himself. But soon after 9/11 shook the nation and President Bush launched his war on terrorism, Rasouli felt rattled to his core. He was haunted by the same type of false political dichotomy that had prompted him to come to America in the first place.

"When the Twin Towers were brought down and, from Ground Zero, George Bush addressed the whole world, telling them, 'If you're not with me, you're against me,' I felt like Saddam was still following me," he said. Despite feeling increasingly uncomfortable in America, he continued to run his business for the time being.

However, in the months after the United States invaded Iraq in 2003, Rasouli became anguished. "I couldn't eat properly, sleep properly, work properly in Minneapolis," he said. He felt his personal sense of identity collapsing. "I really couldn't take it as an American Iraqi or Iraqi American," he said. "The war – the invasion – started within me. I am the Iraqi. At the same time, I am the American. So the American Sami has attacked the Iraqi Sami."

Soon thereafter, he knew he had to make a drastic life change. "I have many family members [in Iraq] . . . so I felt like I betrayed them while I was in the US, watching in my living room the toll of death every day," he said. "Within a year, I decided to go back."

His mind made up, Rasouli began making preparations for his return to his homeland. At a goodbye gathering, he spoke with a Jewish American friend who exhorted him to translate his core convictions into action when he returned to Iraq. "He said, 'Sami, remember, you always wanted to build a bridge for peace – that's your theme here,'" Rasouli said. "So that left an emotional impact on me."

Someone always has to be the first one to start building a bridge. It may feel lonely stepping out and not knowing what to expect – it might even invite ridicule or scoffing – but taking the first step into the unknown makes it easier for others to follow. It also can bring clarity of purpose. That was certainly the case for Rasouli.

About a year after arriving home in Iraq, he met a group of peacemaking activists that traces its roots to its founding in the 1980s by a mix of Mennonites, the Church of the Brethren, and Quakers. The group, known as the Christian Peacemaker Teams, was sending activists to American military encampments "looking for Iraqi young men [captured] by the US," he said. "Their families were worried about them." He soon began traveling with the group to serve as a translator.

"They told me they are in Iraq to tell Iraqis, 'That war is not in our name.' Also, they told me when Jesus Christ was born in Bethlehem, three wise men came [from the East] to the community to tell them about the promise – the promise of peace," Rasouli said. "So we were impressed by their message, their mission in Iraq."

His experience shadowing the Christian Peacemaker Teams helped him find direction. "I wanted to build a bridge of peace, but I had no clue what I'm going to do until I met those guys," Rasouli told me in a video interview from his home in Najaf. "I was born in Iraq, and

I wanted to go there to tell Iraqis that the war – George Bush's war – was not in the name of all Americans. I was telling them my story, but it was tough for me. It was a tough sell. But when I saw the Americans there in Najaf, in Baghdad, in Karbala, in 2005, we were impressed by their mission."

He began to realize that building peaceful bridges between communities that have been torn apart by violence requires a commitment to public service, relationships, and intentional conversation. That's when he formed the Muslim Peacemaker Teams, a group dedicated to bridging divides between Iraqis and building understanding between Americans and Iraqis.

"In the mainstream media of the US, an Arab or Muslim is portrayed as a terrorist," Rasouli said. "In the mainstream media in the Middle East in Arab countries, you find that the Americans or the Europeans or the Westerners are portrayed as infidels. I wanted to bring those terrorists and infidels to a halfway meeting, to come to the table, break the bread, look in the eyes, and find that they are not this or that – all that BS – but they are really brothers and sisters."

Around the same time that Rasouli was starting the Muslim Peacemaker Teams, a loose community of about 20 peace activists in Minneapolis was desperate to do something to counteract some of the damage being done in the war.

The peace activists, including Kathy McKay, "thought it was a terrible overreach invading the country . . . And then all the general population saw on television was suicide bombers," she said. "It became an equation: Iraqis equal suicide bombers. So we were hungry for a way to connect with Iraqis in a human way that was more realistic than just this narrow definition."

That's when they reconnected with Rasouli in an

effort to do something, together, to swim against the tide in their respective countries. "Many, many Americans and Iraqis are misinformed about each other's cultures, and our role comes to bring people together to let them learn about each other," Rasouli said.

In the early going, the Minnesotans didn't know exactly how to help. But Rasouli's group had begun distributing water filters to Iraqi schools as a tangible way to rectify some of the damage done during the Iraqi wars. "The US bombed most of the water plants, so the pipes rusted when there was no water coming through them," McKay said. "Once the plants got back operating, they still didn't have water in the schools." Symbolically and practically, the water filtration project served a very specific purpose. "Water is life," Rasouli said. "And that had an emotional impact on many Americans."

The peacemaking activists in Minneapolis decided to begin sending money for water filtration installation. As their informal fundraising campaign started to pick up momentum, the activists were soon sending several hundred dollars at a time to the Muslim Peacemaker Teams. "The local group here was like, 'If we're going to be sending money, maybe we should be organized. If we're sending money to Iraq, maybe the Treasury Department's going to look at us, [or] the CIA,'" McKay said. "My cavalier attitude was, 'Have them come and look if you want to spend your time and effort investigating. We know who we're sending it to. We're not talking about big money here.'"

But eventually, the activists realized it would be best, at least for tax purposes, to form an official nonprofit. That's what led to the formation of the Iraqi and American Reconciliation Project. The mission of IARP and the Muslim Peacemaker Teams quickly broadened beyond water filtration systems. Soon, IARP was coordinating exhibitions in Minnesota of artwork from a collaborative in Karbala – because art can serve as a vehicle for breaking down cultural divides when conversation and relationships aren't sufficient.

As IARP began gaining attention in Minneapolis, the group sensed an opportunity to press the city to certify the budding local connection to Najaf. McKay, Rasouli, IARP, and their supporters championed a campaign to sign an international partnership naming Minneapolis and Najaf as official Sister Cities.

To many Americans, the Sister Cities International program might seem like nothing more than a municipal government indulgence to fulfill political objectives or to justify international junkets. But to McKay, it means something more. "I'm old enough to remember [President Dwight] Eisenhower, who started the Sister City program," McKay said. "His position was, the militaries of the world are really not going to bring world peace, but person-to-person connections will."

Put into place by the former World War II general, the Sister Cities program turned into a launching point to begin healing relations between the United States and Japan in the years following the war. The first such partnership was sealed between Minneapolis's Twin Cities counterpart of St. Paul and Nagasaki, Japan, in 1955. That was only 10 years after the American military had leveled Nagasaki with an atomic bomb, killing tens of thousands of Japanese people and ending the war. More than six decades later, the United States has more Sister City ties with Japan than with any other nation.[2] The two countries also engage in significant international trade, share cultural connections, and collaborate closely on geopolitical crises.

For McKay, the transformation in relations between the United States and Japan over the course of her lifetime is particularly meaningful because her father served in the military in the Pacific Ocean during the war. The marked shift in attitudes toward the people and culture

of Japan in the years following the war was not foresee-
able when it ended. But over the course of time, "that
totally changed," McKay said. "So I thought, 'Well,
maybe this can happen with Iraq.'"

After IARP's campaign to lobby the Minneapolis City
Council to take action – as well as the endorsement of
local leaders in Najaf – the two cities officially formed
their partnership in 2009.[3] In doing so, they became the
first US–Iraq Sister Cities relationship.

Since then, about 16 delegations of Iraqis have traveled to Minnesota as part of the Sister Cities partnership.
They have formed new relationships that have shattered
misconceptions about each other's personal lives, religious beliefs, and politics.

Building those relationships is especially crucial in
an American political environment in which Muslims,
people of Arabic descent, and Syrian refugees have been
relentlessly demonized. Shortly after Trump took office,
he implemented a travel ban on people from certain
Muslim-majority countries – a directive that originally
included Iraq.[4] "It's become much more mainstream
in the public discourse – the Islamophobes and the
Islamophobic rhetoric – but if you ask Muslim immigrants of Middle Eastern descent if they felt that before
[Trump], they would tell you, 'Yes,'" said Jessica Belt
Saem Eldahr, who became deputy executive director of
IARP in 2015 and took over from McKay as executive
director in 2018. "It's much more out in the open and
accepted a little more. But it was definitely something
we've been dealing with for a long time. It's nothing
new."

Ignorance and intolerance are often fueled by distance, both the physical kind and the metaphorical
kind. When you don't know people on a personal level,
it's easier to hate them. This is a major reason why
Americans are fiercely polarized: we remain isolated
in our chosen social and political groups, clinging to

our relationships with like-minded people instead of embracing ties to people of difference.

"I think a lot of it stems from just fear of the unknown," Belt Saem Eldahr said. "What we hope to do is to bring people together through face-to-face dialogue, or through art, or through some way to lift that veil, if you will, to have them come into a space where it's not so unknown anymore."

Those person-to-person connections that Eisenhower envisioned can break down barriers and transform rhetoric. They are the lifeblood of bridge building. "I think fear dissipates when you meet someone from the Middle East, or a refugee, or a Muslim," Belt Saem Eldahr said. "Just have a friend or have a conversation with someone."

The boxy, aged office building where I met Azar Maluki is tucked away in a nondescript neighborhood in Minneapolis. It's a long walk from the city's bustling downtown, but it's worlds away from the home he left in 2015 to move to America. Soon after arriving in Minneapolis, he joined the board of IARP, believing fervently in the group's mission of generating conversation and relationships as a mechanism to disrupt stereotypes and racism. "Talking to people is very important," he said. "To initiate a dialogue, they can understand, and we can also understand on our side."

Conversations, he said, help undermine conventional wisdom. "Somebody who is isolated and listening to the media – especially the US media or the powerful media in Europe – and have never been in the Middle East or Iraq and start watching these movies of threatening terrorism [and] killing, they start having an aggressive idea about Arabs as a whole. So now comes our turn to explain things to others."

Maluki had his chance to explain things himself

when he staffed IARP's Iraqi culture booth in 2017 at the Festival of Nations in Minneapolis. While manning the display, someone stopped by with an unusual question about life in his home country. "Are you using camels for transportation in Iraq?" the person asked him. Maluki laughed at the memory. "People are not realizing that Iraq" has modern transportation options, brilliant thinkers, and a rich cultural heritage, he said.

Other questions were more serious. "Many people were asking, 'Where does Islam stand on terror or killing other people who have different beliefs and different backgrounds?'" he said. "You start explaining that Islam has nothing to do with these terroristic actions. Terror by itself could originate from any part of the world, regardless of the religion, culture, background, or the country."

To encourage more intentional and meaningful personal connections than the types of ephemeral conversations that are typical in a festival setting, IARP launched a variety of programs under the banner of "People to People." The programs, which reached more than 40,000 people in 2018, include potlucks, picnics, speakers, and excursions for groups of Iraqis and Americans.[5] Women's friendship groups have also been formed as part of the People to People initiative, bringing together Iraqi and American women for monthly gatherings to promote interaction and conversation.

When I met with McKay in Minneapolis, her latest women's friendship group had just wrapped up. "We were women together cooking and having food and meeting in each other's homes, and then we went to places," she said. "We went to the Capitol one time, and then we went to a museum and some big parks and things like that. We all learned about one another's children and grandchildren, and sometimes somebody would bring a child with them."

The women of McKay's group made a point of attending an Iftar celebration together – an after-sunset meal that's part of Islam's Ramadan tradition. "The non-Muslims all mostly came to that – and then during the Christian holiday, we had a Christmas party meal at a home where all the Christmas decorations were up, and many of the Iraqi women were really curious and appreciated that," McKay said. "So it's sharing cultures back and forth."

There's not necessarily a specific agenda or conversation topic at the women's friendship groups. "What we do is try to create shared spaces for organic conversations. It's not very forced," she said. "It's more about, 'Let's come together at a table and eat a meal together.' Naturally, [there are] conversations that chip away at negative stereotypes, or these ideas of the 'other' that you have in your head."

The communal characteristics of having a meal together create the foundation for the type of conversation and relationship building that do not typically occur between people of difference. "I think you have to find the shared space," McKay said. "What are the connection points – finding those spaces that both communities or the individuals might feel familiar with. It's accessible to them. It's safe for them to come."

From a purely practical perspective, when people share their preferred cuisine with each other, bonds are formed. There's something genuine and simply human about the entire experience. "Come and bring your dish that speaks to your background. You share it with someone and get to taste someone else's dish. It's quite simple," Belt Saem Eldahr said. "You find the places where there are connections or similar interests and go from there."

Those types of settings open up the door for reconciliation. "I don't think you can move on and heal unless you feel that you've been heard, and you've expressed the pain and how it's impacted you, and feel that the other person understands," she said. "Then you can hopefully take steps toward healing. But I don't think that can really take place unless there's some understanding there."

Personal interaction and conversation can build understanding, but sometimes that's not enough. Recognizing that, IARP leaders believed they could use alternative forms of communication to achieve their mission, as well. More than a decade ago, the organization formed the Iraqi Art Project to showcase works that seek to broaden cultural understanding, which included the display of works by Karbala artists.

"Art has a way of facilitating dialogue around difficult conversations that might be hard to have in just a direct way," Belt Saem Eldahr said. "You're able to come at it in different stages in your journey toward change. You could come and have it be more of a passive experience, where you're viewing art and having an internal dialogue. You can engage with it at different levels. And then I think it just moves you in different ways."

Soon after joining IARP, Belt Saem Eldahr began discussing new methods of using art to communicate across cultural boundaries. "We engaged the local Iraqi community in what art form they wanted to access to share their stories," she said. "We had done books. We had done film. What was something new they want to learn about and share their stories through?"

Theater surfaced as a compelling medium for the group's purposes. "Hearing someone's story through a conversation might not impact you as much as through a theater experience," she said. "It engages different senses, and you're able to address topics or issues that are harder to talk about in other ways."

In 2017, IARP introduced its first theatrical production, *Birds Sing Differently*, which tells the true story of 12 Iraqi refugees and immigrants living in Minnesota. "It touches on themes like home, loss, fear, grief in a way that I think is true to their stories," Belt Saem Eldahr said. The end result, the product of a year of development, included Iraqi natives in leading roles. "They're sharing it themselves," she said.

The production debuted to a sold-out crowd at the Guthrie Theater in Minneapolis and went on a statewide tour in 2019. "When I saw the play at the Guthrie Theater, I thought it was so real, and it was just from heart to heart – from the hearts of Iraqis to the hearts of Americans and everybody else," Maluki said. "I believe that art is one of the important ways of communication. There's something interesting in everybody's soul, regardless of where he's living, the East or West. It's a fast and effective way of communication. Everybody could explain what he's feeling in a way that he couldn't explain through talking or through dialogue."

The general audience reaction to *Birds Sing Differently* demonstrated the power of theater to reach others. "The feedback we got from the audience was, 'I never thought about what it was like,' 'I never saw it this way before,'" McKay said. "People were very impacted."

While one of IARP's principal goals is fostering better understanding among Americans of the Iraqi people and their culture, the group also aims to educate the Iraqi community about the American people and their culture. Those interactions facilitate a fresh perspective on both sides, Maluki said. "When you start engaging the American people, things start not only to change but to shift in a positive direction. Many, many Iraqis start to realize that there are two distinct things – there are the American people and the American government. They both have different ideas and different behavior toward

Iraq. This was totally absent during the time of war. This was a big change in understanding the nature of the American culture and the American people."

The US invasion of Iraq can still be a contentious topic, generating debate about the Bush administration's motivations, strategy, and policies, as well as the insurgency tactics of Iraqi militants. So when IARP promotes interaction, it emphasizes the shared humanity between Americans and Iraqis in the hope of fueling better understanding over time on the tougher issues. "We are trying most of the time to speak on the human level – from human to human," Maluki said. "We feel that is a much better way for understanding and for communicating with others."

Those interpersonal connections are making a difference because authentic relationships spark change in people's hearts. "Giving each other respect, tolerance, and understanding – this is a big achievement," Maluki said. "This is a big victory – not a victory of the war, but we have an old statement in Iraq that 'bad things may give rise to many good things in the future.' And that's what happened after the war. Because of the war, we got to know each other. I have very loyal friends like [Jessica], Kathy, and many others. I think these personal relationships are a big achievement."

To be sure, the cultivation of conversation and relationships doesn't involve the erasure of differences. It does not involve cultural assimilation – in fact, quite the opposite. It translates into acceptance, understanding, and genuine connections rooted in truth. "It's about being heard," Belt Saem Eldahr said.

The Iraqis and the Americans who interact with each other through IARP don't necessarily agree on the geopolitical issues that continue to affect the relationship between their countries. But sharing difficult truths with each other is a form of bridge building that gets noisy. It often involves disagreements – and that's normal.

"You just have to accept that there are going to be people who are going to differ on things you feel strongly about," Belt Saem Eldahr said. "But you still have to engage with them. In our community, we have refugees, immigrants, peace activists, professional students. There's a wide range of perspectives. But I think we can come [together] around some of the facts or the things that we can agree on."

And even if you can't agree on the facts, the pursuit of reconciliation does not have to stop. "That's the point of our work is to bring people into the process and say, 'You can be a part of this. You can participate,'" Belt Saem Eldahr said. "It's a journey. It's not like, oh, one day it's going to be reconciled."

I asked Maluki a question that I asked many others I interviewed for this book: is reconciliation a process that can be learned? "I believe so," he replied. "Maybe we can ask the question the other way around: can love be learned? Yes, of course. Because love lies in the heart of everybody."

Despite the injustices that have been perpetuated on his homeland by both insiders and outsiders – injustices that cannot be washed away with a conversation or a theatrical performance – and despite the feeling of helplessness that was, at times, virtually inescapable, Maluki has not lost his faith in the fundamental goodness of humankind to mend brokenness.

"The issue is that we need some time to polish it, to bring it to the surface," he said. "All people have love, but they don't know how to use it. The good part of every human being is much more than the bad parts."

3

From Hating to Healing

Even in death, racism is alive.

That much is inescapable at Oakwood Cemetery in Charlottesville, Virginia, whose legacy of prejudice and inequity is still vivid more than a century and a half after the sprawling graveyard was established. The cemetery was racially segregated for several decades after its initiation in 1863, when Virginia was fighting with the Confederacy to preserve slavery.

When I visited in January 2019, a haunting glow illuminated the graveyard's weathered tombstones as the sun dipped below the horizon on a nearly cloudless winter day. American flags were sprinkled throughout the plots, along with a smattering of red poinsettias left over from Christmas.

Directly across the street to the north is another cemetery, much smaller and noticeably less grand – this one established about a decade after Oakwood to provide the town's African American residents with a proper place to rest. The Daughters of Zion, a group of Black women dedicated to playing a charitable role in Reconstruction following the Civil War, started the Daughters of Zion Cemetery as a resolute counterweight to its exclusionary neighbor. As many as 300 souls were laid to rest there from 1873 through 1995. Only half of their identities are known.[1]

Glancing southward through the gaps in Oakwood's leafless, wind-tossed branches, I could see Mt. Zion First African Baptist Church in the distance. Panes of blue-and-purple stained-glass windows came into view on the eastern side of the church building. Their beauty was muted as sunbeams deflected off the western side of the building. But the stained glass nonetheless retained its countenance of resilience.

Inside the church, the Rev. Alvin Edwards shuffled through the hallways in a bright-red long-sleeved shirt, slacks, and black socks paired with sporty flip-flops – the comfort-first outfit of someone who has called this place home for more than three decades. The longtime pastor of Mt. Zion was busily making preparations for a gathering later that evening of the Charlottesville Clergy Collective, which he founded.

His appointment as a conduit of healing and reconciliation in this broken community was nothing if not divine. Yet it was certainly not inevitable.

Years before Charlottesville played host in August 2017 to a hate-filled rally of White supremacists that culminated in the public murder of a young demonstrator and attracted worldwide attention, Edwards wanted to begin building bridges between people of difference in his community. He had visions of starting a group to begin whittling away at the community's edifice of White privilege and racism. So he figured there was no better place to begin than the realm of faith, which had historically been used as an instrument of division in a town that was not far removed from slavery and Jim Crow.

So Edwards picked up the phone one day, some years before the Charlottesville attack, and called a clerical colleague, who was White, from another local church. "I asked about having World Communion Sunday together," he recalled. "The pastor said he'd get back with me. Well, it went and it passed. And he never said a word."

The other pastor's silence was an obvious "no." Edwards later confronted his colleague. "I suggested something we could do to get together, and you just completely ignored it," Edwards told him. His colleague was not interested in forming the type of relationship and having the type of difficult conversations that might begin to break down the barriers that continued to socially, politically, and economically segregate the people of Charlottesville. "He didn't want to do it," Edwards said.

Discouraged, Edwards set aside his plans to launch an interfaith ministry in hopes of disrupting the void of community that was festering in Charlottesville. But in 2015, he was deeply shaken when a White supremacist opened fire at the historic Emanuel African Methodist Episcopal Church in Charleston, South Carolina, slaughtering nine Black parishioners with the aim of sparking a race war.[2]

The Charleston shooting gave Edwards the resolve to resume his efforts to pursue healing in Charlottesville. He began calling his fellow faith leaders, one by one, to ignite conversation about the need for them to begin bridging divides in the community. One of his first calls was to Michael Cheuk, who was then serving as the senior pastor at Charlottesville's University Baptist Church. Cheuk, whose family immigrated to America from Hong Kong in the 1970s, had increasingly felt like he was pastoring his largely White church from an island.

"I was beginning to feel that I needed to be out in the community more," he said. "Even as I preach about how God wants the church to be outside of its own walls, God was telling me, 'Michael, this is an opportunity.'"

That opportunity coalesced in the form of the Charlottesville Clergy Collective, launched by Edwards in 2016 to enable local faith leaders to begin forming relationships and discussing issues that had long divided them, including matters involving race. In their first meeting together, Edwards struck a somber tone. "If Charleston had happened in Charlottesville, how many of you think I would've called you?" Edwards asked his clerical colleagues. His inquiry lingered uncomfortably in the air. Nobody spoke up.

"And the answer was, 'None of you,'" Edwards said. "Well, why? A couple people said, 'I don't know you.' And that was it. They don't know me. I don't know you."

They lacked the type of authentic relationships that are necessary to build bridges. But that would soon change.

⋰⋰⋰

In the initial months following the formation of the Charlottesville Clergy Collective, members had few concrete objectives except the pursuit of friendships. They simply didn't know each other well – or, in some cases, at all. Members went on periodic one-on-one lunch dates together. Their assignment: to learn about each other on a personal level. "The purpose was to fellowship, and it was a safe place where we could talk about things," Edwards said.

That type of safe space is particularly needed for religious leaders because of the spiritual chasms that continue to divide people of faith. Trust between leaders from different Christian denominations and between leaders from different religions altogether is scarce. When I interviewed Edwards for this book, he had just returned from a retreat where he'd heard talk of a recent incident in which a Black pastor in Georgia had swapped pulpits with a White pastor for one Sunday in a spirit of unity. "After they swapped pulpits, they both got fired," Edwards said.

His fear was that something like that could happen to the members of his burgeoning group in Charlottesville.

But that fear is precisely why the group is needed, said the Rev. Brenda Brown-Grooms, the African American co-pastor of Charlottesville's diverse New Beginnings Christian Community Church and a member of the collective.

Born in Charlottesville, Brown-Grooms lived there in her youth but left the area for college, spending time in New York and Nashville before returning to her home-town in her fifties, a little over a decade ago, in a pastoral capacity. She speaks with the passion and authority that comes from years of chasing justice amidst inequity.

"I left thinking I would come back when I was very, very, very old. And God tricked me and sent me back far sooner than I thought," she said, chuckling. "Home is always nice, but the first thing I thought when I came back was, 'Oh, my gosh, they're doing things exactly the same. That's not good.'"

Racism was still plainly evident in her hometown. "Why I was back?" she asked rhetorically. "I went around the world only to come back here to have to fight the fight I was always going to have to fight. C'mon, God." She laughed again, this time with a degree of spiritual resignation. "God's rather insistent," she said, making pointed eye contact with me.

The fight, Brown-Grooms concluded, would have to begin with the pursuit of relationships. And for mem-bers of the clergy, those relationships would have to begin with genuine personal connection and conversa-tion. "We have to have a safe space. I believe that the work of this generation is to figure out how to talk about the hard issues because we're out of time if we don't figure out how to talk to each other."

Lacking bridges to foster those conversations, we often refuse to even engage with people of difference because we want to avoid difficult discussions in the first place. We'd rather stay on our side of the ravine. This is particularly the case for White people like me, who often continue to capitalize on the chasms separating them from people of color.

Brown-Grooms paused for a moment, arched her eyebrows, and launched into an impression of a dainty Southern accent. "We can be very polite," she said, raising her voice an extra octave and holding a wide smile. "You don't bring up nasty or inappropriate things. This miscegenation problem and then integration and all of that – they are not polite conversation, my son, all right? You're supposed to be nice," she continued, dragging the "i" for emphasis. "Have some tea. Would you like some cookies?"

She cut off the accent. "This patina of foolishness is shining over the real mess," she said. "But what we've discovered is what we know as pastors anyway: for the people to do it, we've got to do it first." That is, if faith leaders want their parishioners to span the political, social, racial, and religious gaps that divide them, the leaders themselves must first do the same thing. They must set the example. They must have the same conversations. And they must confront their own biases and the role their churches have played in perpetuating painful gulfs in their communities.

But those realizations could not take place in Charlottesville without first establishing an atmosphere of intentional community among local faith leaders despite their many differences. "If you're going to act together, you have to know one another and know who you can trust. You've got to know who's serious, who's not, how they think about things," said Rabbi Tom Gutherz of Charlottesville's only synagogue, Congregation Beth Israel, and a member of the collective. "We invested time to get to know one another."

One of the group's immediate priorities was to contemplate the role of local faith institutions in fueling racism in Charlottesville. A group like the collective functions as "one little piece" of what needs to be a broader effort to confront White supremacy, Gutherz said. "There's activists, and they've got a role. There's politicians, there's academics, there's community organizers. Everybody's got to do their part," he said. "We're not all going to do the same thing. But we all need one another to do what we're doing, so we can't be stabbing each other in the back."

For the members of the Charlottesville Clergy Collective, their goal was to use their "deep reach into the community" to serve as a "prophetic witness," guiding residents toward truth and reconciliation, Gutherz said. In the first year following the Charleston mass shooting, the collective hadn't necessarily fixed anything. But that wasn't the point. Rather, the group had achieved a degree of cohesion that did not previously exist. Construction was in progress.

"We were coming together," Brown-Grooms said.

⚬⚬⚬⚬⚬

The winds of hate were blowing in Charlottesville months before racist demonstrators took to the streets in their "Unite the Right" rally promoting White supremacy and xenophobia.

"The faith community was among the first to recognize the storm that definitely was going to come," Brown-Grooms said. "It's interesting how God works. We were in place, so we wouldn't have to get in place when all of that began to happen – because you couldn't even imagine trying to do all of the work in the months before. Oh, gosh." She touched her dark-red horn-rimmed glasses as she gathered her composure. "The Clergy Collective group – whether we knew it or not at the time – had already done the groundwork necessary to attempt to take on the onslaught that happened in the summer of 2017," she said.

The storm had begun to brew when the Charlottesville City Council announced it was weighing proposals to strip two public parks of their Confederate names[3] and to remove a statue of Confederate General Robert E. Lee from the one bearing his name.[4] Soon after those plans hit the docket, racist groups began plotting to flood the city with hate.

At Congregation Beth Israel, members arrived on the morning of Saturday, May 14, for their Shabbat service, a weekly tradition on the Jewish day of rest. They quickly noticed commotion across the street in a park named after Confederate General Stonewall Jackson, whose name was among those poised for removal by the City Council.

The bronze monument displayed in the park, featuring Jackson saddled triumphantly on a warhorse, had been installed in 1921 in a celebration organized by the local chapters of the Confederate Veterans, Sons of Confederate Veterans, and Daughters of the Confederacy. Some 5,000 people had paraded through the streets to celebrate the statue's installation, with schoolchildren arranging themselves as "a living representation of the Confederate flag." Stonewall Jackson's great-great-granddaughter, Anna Jackson Preston, whose mother was living in Charlottesville at the time, attended the gathering to commemorate her ancestor's legacy.[5]

White nationalist Richard Spencer descended on the park to do the same thing 96 years later, leading a hate-filled demonstration of his own in honor of Stonewall Jackson.[6] The stunned members of Congregation Beth Israel watched the whole thing play out through a window of their synagogue.

It was just the beginning. Two months later, about 50 members of the Ku Klux Klan, including some in white robes, picked the city for a public demonstration.[7] There was no significant violence at Spencer's rally or the KKK demonstration, but the threat of an eruption was becoming increasingly visceral. "That really got our attention," Cheuk said.

Rabia Povich, vice president of the Charlottesville Clergy Collective and a minister with the Inayati Universal Sufi Order, said it was becoming evident that the collective would need to move beyond conversation and into action. "The degree to which division and hate was being promoted in segments of our society, of our country, of Charlottesville, was part of it," said Povich, who is White. "It was something we could feel – the political divisions, the social divisions, the economic divisions, and the racial and religious divisions. To me, this is the opposite of the essence of spirituality, the essence of faith, of God. We can see that we need to be vocal about building bridges by holding a strong moral tone."

In a gathering on the eastern edge of Charlottesville's picturesque Downtown Mall on July 8, 2017, Gutherz sent a message of love, even as the KKK descended on the town. "This [is] our answer to those who come here to preach hate and exclusion and supremacy," he proclaimed. Three words in Hebrew from Psalm 89 crystallized the message: *olam hesed yibaneh*, which, he said, can be translated in several ways and inspired his message for Charlottesville:

> I will build this world from love
> And you will build this world from love
> And if we build this world from love
> Then God will build this world from love.[8]

For Charlottesville – home to Monticello, the estate of Declaration of Independence writer, president, and slaveholder Thomas Jefferson – and for Virginia – whose history of slavery, segregation, and intolerance remains visible in its cemeteries, parks, neighborhoods, and textbooks – the events of 2017 were not throwbacks to the past. They were reflective of the painful present.

"It was an uncovering for some of us of the injustices that had been perpetuated systemically against people of color and discrimination that had been perpetuated against Jewish people, as well," Povich said. "Thomas Jefferson's . . . great words were written here with the assistance of . . . enslaved people who helped him at Monticello and . . . on his multiple properties. His great thinking couldn't have been done without [people who were enslaved]. This is [Charlottesville's] foundation. It's time to be honest and say, 'Damage has been done for hundreds of years, and repair hasn't happened.'"

Brown-Grooms said the extremist demonstrators clearly drew inspiration from the election and divisive rhetoric of Donald Trump, whom she referred to not by name but instead by his slot in the order of American presidents. "Many things started coming into focus after the election of 45," she said. "There were immediate jumps, in my remembrance, of not just anti-Semitism but the continuing attack on people of color, on immigrants. I think people of faith were particularly attuned because you could feel it. Unless something happens to stop our going – as a people, a country, a community – in a particular direction, there's going to be some kind of manifestation. That's the prophetic end of ministry. If we're plugged in right, we feel when there's something evil coming."

As Charlottesville braced for the "Unite the Right" rally in August 2017, members of the collective wanted to do something to counteract the historic role of the Christian faith in enabling, encouraging, propagating, or ignoring hate and inequity. But how could a group of people who were still grappling with their own religious and political conflicts take action in a spirit of unity?

"We were just designed for conversation – but we were pushed into action," Cheuk said. "It also raised up differences in philosophy and strategy and tactics. And we really had to wrestle with how [to] respond in a way that is both authentic . . . but still as a group so that we don't fracture."

Eventually, the members agreed that public demonstrations could serve as a unifying force despite their theological, political, and cultural differences. When it became clear that White supremacists were preparing to leave an explosive mark, the collective members staked out the place where the rally was set to occur. "We did a prayer walk," Cheuk said. "And we allowed and encouraged various people from different traditions to lead in ways that were consonant and rooted in their own tradition."

A subset of the group also carved out a role as peaceful counter-protestors. They organized a march that Saturday morning ahead of the combustible rally in the afternoon, beginning at the Jefferson School City Center and then marching around the area where the White supremacists' rally would later erupt into violence.[9]

"Get out, this is our town, you're not welcome here, you're not wanted here, your hate speech has no place here, and we will not allow you to come in and oppress us," march organizer Don Gathers said during the rally, according to a local news report. "We will not allow you to intimidate us, we won't allow you to come in and take our town over."[10]

Their pleas were swept aside by the White nationalist demonstrators – including neo-Nazis and multiple groups with ties to extreme right-wing, racist ideologies[11] – who swarmed Charlottesville that afternoon and clashed with a group of counter-protestors promoting messages of love and acceptance. When a White supremacist sped his car into a throng of counter-protestors, killing 32-year-old Heather Heyer and injuring others, the horrifying images circulated instantaneously on social media and were showcased on news broadcasts.[12] It was an excruciating visual depiction of the legacy of hate, and it was stark evidence that extremism had been emboldened in the aftermath of Trump's ascent to the White House.

In the wake of the attack, local leaders in Charlottesville, concerned about the reputational effects on their community, scrambled to portray the events as the antithesis of the town's welcoming spirit. "I remember immediately afterward, all the city [leaders] wanted to do a publicity campaign that Charlottesville was 'a great place – come back,'" Gutherz said. "The line was, 'These are all people from outside.' And technically that might have been true. But actually, people said, 'Wait, wait, wait a second. Not so fast.'"

"This is us," Brown-Grooms said.

"I think those who were paying attention said, 'Hey . . . this isn't just people from outside [Charlottesville],'" Gutherz continued.

For healing and reconciliation to begin to occur, they said, the town needed to undertake an honest exploration of its racist roots – and that honest discussion could finally begin to take place because the members of the collective were in place to lead it. "There's something socially and morally larger that we have to speak to, whether people have faith or not," Povich said. "It's not all healed. It's not all taken care of. People can get angry and speak to each other in anger and in pain but not with hate, knowing that we can educate each other and that I, as one, am willing to be educated about how we can better live our lives."

But can people really change? Can people who have demonstrated racism or bigotry learn how to accept, appreciate, edify, and stand up for people of color and others of difference?

The Rev. Alvin Edwards believes they can. "I remain hopeful because I'm a firm believer that people's hearts can change," he said. "No matter what they've done, what their history, what their past is, I believe they can change." Your opinion on whether others can change isn't a commentary on what you believe about others. It's actually a reflection on what you believe about yourself. "I have to believe that," Edwards continued, "because, see, the belief that people cannot change means I cannot change."

~~~~~~~~

Offering prayers and standing up to hate and starting a conversation were good first steps for the members of the Charlottesville Clergy Collective. But these steps were also, by the members' own admission, insufficient. To grapple with the legacy of hate, which trained an international magnifying glass on Charlottesville, the members felt an urgency to trek beyond the city's boundaries to learn more about the confluence of forces that led to the town's fateful summer. "The uncovering of history is really a big piece of what we need to do," Gutherz said.

One major obstacle in the road to bridge building is a lack of education about basic history. Bridge building requires an authentic examination and exposure of old wounds and ongoing inequities that continue to undermine the pursuit of community and reconciliation. Ignoring the truth will only lead to structural failure before the bridge can even open for traffic. When it comes to racism, this speaks directly to the need for White people to shed their ignorance about America's history of discrimination and brutality against people of color.

Becoming aware of history is just as important to metaphorical bridge builders as education is to people who build real-life bridges. Would you want to drive over a bridge designed by an untrained architect? Knowledge matters.

"I was a history teacher. I love history. I read history – in my free time, I read it – and there's so much I didn't know about," Gutherz said. He never realized how much he didn't know until he began an intentional quest to discover more. "And if that was the case for me, imagine [what it's like] for people who don't even have a feeling for history," he said. "It just makes me realize that the work is really, really huge."

That doesn't mean people can't have disagreements over the implications of truth or various aspects of the facts. Healthy disagreement is a natural element of bridge building. The members of the Charlottesville Clergy Collective acknowledged that they still have significant disagreements over theology and politics and racism. "Best arguments in the world," Brown-Grooms said, laughing. But, as leaders, they can have those difficult conversations because of the relationships they've formed. "Conflict is neither positive nor negative. It is. What's negative or positive is how we deal with it," Brown-Grooms said. It's how you respond to each other that decides whether the bridge collapses before it's even open for traffic or stays upright and operational.

"By building those relationships, not only do we understand more about the world and about people, we also get to trust," Gutherz said. "That, I think, allows us to disagree. We've got issues that are clearly divisive."

But they are devoted to understanding each other because they care about each other. "We have made a commitment to exploring everyone's experience with racism and injustice and privilege – whatever it is," he said. And sometimes confrontation is necessary when differences arise. "I kind of want to get in your face with it so that we can address it," Edwards said. "I just want them to feel like you're in a safe place."

When relationships are in place before the conversation begins, each person involved in the give-and-take is much more likely to approach the exchange with an attitude of introspection. "I try to be really clear that the other person has his or her own junk and struggle, and I'm going to work on my own," Cheuk said. "So if that person triggers me, my first question is not, 'Why is he such a jerk?' but, 'Why am I being triggered?' That has been really helpful for me to get past my tribal lens. I already have judged them before even knowing them. But if I can just take that step back, that's been really helpful."

⁘⁘⁘

In July 2018, multiple members of the collective, including Gutherz and Brown-Grooms, joined about 100 people from the Charlottesville community for a bus trip to hotspots of racism, inequity, and violence throughout the South. About one-third of the group was made up of low-income adult residents, another quarter were high school students and teachers, and the rest included county leaders, city officials, a cohort from the University of Virginia, and the clergy.

Their first stop was to a seemingly unremarkable patch of property on the outskirts of town. There, historians had recently discovered, a Black man named John Henry James was ripped by a mob from a police escort train in 1898, lynched on a tree, and riddled with bullets after he was accused of assaulting an unmarried White woman.[13]

"Since God works in mysterious ways, it happened to be on the property of a country club that did not admit Jewish people or African Americans for many, many years," Gutherz said. "And they graciously – after some indication of what it would look like if they refused – agreed to let us gather there."

When he was murdered, James had been on his way to face a trial for his alleged crimes. Even after his lynching, he was convicted by a grand jury.[14] But no one was ever charged for his death.[15]

"We began by gathering some earth from the site of the lynching of John Henry James," Gutherz later wrote in a blog post. "We wanted to give John Henry James a place in the memory of our town."

As the travelers continued on their journey of contemplation and education, they visited Confederate monuments and civil rights sites in Appomattox, Virginia; Danville, Virginia; Greensboro, North Carolina; Charlotte, North Carolina; Atlanta, Georgia; Birmingham, Alabama; Montgomery, Alabama; and Selma, Alabama. Along the way, the group toured museums and met with local activists to learn.[16]

"Every place that we went, we had in the back of our minds, 'What is the story? How is this story being told? And what's being concealed?'" Gutherz said. "With the idea of coming back from that and saying, 'How are we going to tell our story after having seen all the things that we saw?'"

For Brown-Grooms, the trip brought her face to face with a painful narrative perpetuated by educators during her youth. "I remember being a little girl and being in a Virginia history class, and I said, 'There weren't no happy slaves, what are you talking about?' I thought, 'Who's telling this story? They're telling it wrong. They're not telling it the way my mom and grandmother and grandpapa told me. So why are you telling the story differently? Who benefits from it being told this way? Who does not? Who's in power?'" Building bridges, she said, requires understanding whose stories have been excluded and then retelling their stories "with everybody's part included."

Perhaps the most meaningful moments on the pilgrimage came in periods of reflection, together, in the caravan. "And as much as I hate traveling on buses . . . what was holy and sacred for me was all the people on the buses with me and the time we spent," Brown-Grooms said. "We experienced that all together. No matter what they espoused, all of our hearts were touched, and we created a community." The relationships they forged formed the foundation for reconciliation. She walked away from the trip with a firm hope. "The thought was to be seeds that come back and get planted in this community," she said. "And let's see what grows up – a different narrative, a different understanding of the history that we all share."

As they went from place to place, they carried the soil from the ground where James was murdered. "It was just one person. But it's what we had. One life, one experience – that's a paradigm for the experience of so many people," Gutherz said. "We were able to, with holy context, bring him to a place where he was going to be honored and recognized and named. It just felt like a holy act."

"It was," Brown-Grooms said.

They could not bury racism – because you cannot bury that which is alive – but, together, they could grapple honestly with its legacy.

As they contemplated the life and death of John Henry James, the rabbi's thoughts dwelt on the story of how the Ark of the Covenant sustained the people of Israel as they wandered the wilderness. "It is not the people who carry the Ark, it is the Ark that carries the people," he wrote after the trip. "It struck me that it was not we who were carrying the soil; the soil – which represented our desire to speak more truthfully about our history, to face the future with a commitment to make amends, and to move towards justice and healing – was carrying us."[17]

Part II

Reconnecting with Truth

In the digital age, we have witnessed a swift transfer of power from the old guards of news and information to a new form of gatekeepers. The professional print journalists and broadcasters who once vetted and curated most of the emerging information about the world that people encountered on a regular basis have declined considerably in size and influence. While newspapers such as the *New York Times* and networks such as CBS retain significant influence over the news diet of millions of Americans, the reality is that mainstream media outlets have lost their once-tight grip on our daily news consumption habits. The news is now beholden to tech companies that employ sophisticated algorithms to present to Americans customized feeds of information based on previous indicators of what those users *want* to see – not what they *need* to see.

This stands in stark contrast to the journalistic values of recent decades, when, despite the many flaws of the news industry – not the least of which was a lack of diversity that led to the news being filtered through the perspective of mostly White male editors – the primary creed held that the truth matters most, regardless of whether it was what Americans wanted to encounter. And encounter it they did – because there simply weren't many viable alternatives. Daily newspapers and network evening news broadcasts kept most Americans on the same page regarding the facts. Journalists operated based on the core principle that it was their job to help Americans sort fact from fiction and to avoid absurd conspiracy theories that might otherwise disrupt democracy.

To be sure, this remains the central tenet of most major mainstream media outlets. In my job at *USA Today*, I am responsible for delivering accurate and authoritative reports by assessing the legitimacy of my sources, validating information provided to me, and presenting a coherent and authentic narrative that helps readers understand the world around them and live their lives accordingly. Regrettably, however, I am among a dying breed. While I expect powerhouses like the *New York Times*, the *Washington Post*, the *Wall Street Journal*, and *USA Today* to live on, local news organizations and even many large news outlets have been swiftly shrinking for years. Essentially, every journalist I know has worked for publications that have experienced layoffs, implemented huge budget cuts, reduced print days, or all of the above. That includes me. Three of the six newspapers I've worked for no longer exist, and I was only 36 years old at the time of this writing. Even as I was writing this book, several of my journalist friends were laid off, and I was personally placed on several unpaid weeks of furlough due to the industry's financial issues. Around the same time, the stocks of Google[1] and Facebook[2] hit all-time highs.

The diminishment of traditional media outlets has, of course, corresponded with the rise of Google, Facebook, Twitter, Instagram, and other tech platforms that have built their businesses in part on the backs of news that has been distributed for free by outlets like mine. But their Silicon Valley values stand in stark contrast to those of traditional journalists, and this collision of principles has wreaked havoc on the relationship between Americans and the facts. Rather than placing the truth at the center of what they do, social media companies prioritize engagement – a fuzzy metric fed by likes, comments, replies, shares, and clicks. As you have surely seen, the more engaging posts tend to be the more sensational ones, including memes that enrage, comments that inspire fury, links that spur anger, and retweets that cultivate contempt. The posts that present a warped portrait of others often flourish, skewing our perceptions of each other and causing us to be more and more polarized. Content containing authentic explorations of complex issues and promoting contemplation is often buried because it does not generate enough attention. Thoughtfulness doesn't generate profits for tech companies. Instead, they generate profits by capitalizing on our human attraction to eye-popping content, coupled with our normal tendency to congregate with like-minded people and to engage in confirmation bias. Feeding stuff to us online that reiterates our beliefs about people who aren't like us simply exacerbates our crisis of affective polarization. Instead of professional journalists curating the news, our closest friends – people who share similar life experiences and similar perspectives about the world – are effectively curating the news for us, since it's their posts that show up in our feeds. Naturally, we tend to share content that raises suspicions about or demonizes those who aren't like us.

The result is that many of the bridges, if you will, that once connected Americans with the truth about the world around them have imploded. In their place, we have a litany of structurally unsound alternatives. Amid the collapse in revenue for traditional media, numerous new outlets have sprung onto the scene, delivering highly partisan material that simmers in the dark corners of social media, where trolls and gotcha artists attack and shame. Since they are not constrained by the facts, nor by the social media companies that enable them to flourish, their misleading content has become a mainstay in our digital feeds and inboxes. As a result, while legitimate questions have emerged about the validity of content on these partisan sites, those concerns have been overtaken by illegitimate accusations that mainstream outlets are spreading "fake news," further eroding trust in authentic journalism. During his presidency, of course, Donald Trump himself was the leading proponent of harmful and inaccurate allegations of "fake news" against outlets like the *New York Times* and CNN. And given the grouping effect of politics, which creates an us-versus-them mentality, his allegations resonated for his supporters. He also perpetually spread misinformation through tweets and interviews, amounting to more than 22,000 "false or misleading claims" as of early September 2020, according to a *Washington Post* database.[3] The end result of Trump's consistent stream of falsehoods is a sizable portion of the American electorate predisposed to distrust journalists more than ever.

I'll always defend the role of mainstream media against bogus and irresponsible accusations of "fake news." To be fair, however, a thorough autopsy on the death of facts would not render our industry as altogether blameless. Under financial pressure, certain bad actors in our industry have responded by allowing digital metrics to seize control of decision-making, a slippery slope that often elevates clickbait and leads to the deterioration of trust among readers. We, as a news industry, need to reexamine the ways in which we have failed to properly serve our readers when we have chosen trending news over authentic portraits of complex issues. We need to confront our soundbite culture, embrace nuance, and refuse to allow the rapid news cycle to wipe out coverage of important issues. Politicians like Trump were born to capitalize on a wickedly fast news culture that emphasizes spontaneity and sensationalism over complexity and context. This includes people on both sides of the political aisle. But we, as journalists, can still choose to prioritize substance and depth – which, despite conventional wisdom, can be presented in engaging ways that attract readership and viewership.

Likewise, we need to confront the fact that the demise of small-town journalism has left a vacuum of local news in communities throughout America, eroding trust between readers and journalists and further weakening the news industry's reputation despite our best intentions to continue serving as a beacon of truth. How can we expect people to trust journalists if they don't even know any? Addressing this will require further investments by the philanthropic community and others in sustainable nonprofit journalism ventures that are not bound by the same financial pressures as corporate media.

To be clear, social media is here to stay, and there's no point in denying it. And that's not altogether bad. Online news and social media *can* be a source of togetherness, not division, when specifically designed to serve that purpose. Any doubts that Facebook, Twitter, and other social networking sites could serve as an instigator of change should have been erased when they served as the platform through which the video of George Floyd's killing first reached the public, spurring a movement against racism in cities throughout America. Indeed, that instance and others like it demonstrate the occasionally productive role of social media in promoting transparency among the major institutions in our lives. But for every example of social media playing a positive part in our democratic discourse, there are countless others of how social media has catalyzed division and hate, often via misinformation.

And it will almost surely get worse. After Trump's defeat in 2020, several networking services designed to appeal to far-right conservatives – including Parler, MeWe, and Gab – began to flourish, gaining millions of followers within days.[4] Their appeal is based on their anti-censorship pledge never to remove or limit the spread of content containing misinformation after Facebook and Twitter placed warning labels on many of Trump's posts and removed other lies about the election, both during the campaign and in the days following Joe Biden's victory. The ideological bifurcation of social media would simply exacerbate our crisis of political tribalism, further separating Americans from people who don't look, think, or believe like them.

What we need is a fundamental reset of how Americans interact with news and information. What we need, in fact, is a bridge building approach to fact-checking, journalism, and social media. The truth, when presented through strategically designed media, can serve as a bridge that connects Americans with each other. Our democracy depends on the free flow of accurate news and trust in its production, distribution, and presentation. And it depends on equipping Americans with the ability to engage deeply with reliable digital information, rather than digging into dangerous conspiracy theories like QAnon or mindlessly grazing personalized and polarizing content.

As I said in the Introduction to this book, simply bashing people over the head with the facts isn't enough to get them on the same page if the facts contradict their views about the world. But if the facts are communicated in a way that leverages trusted relationships, the truth can reach its intended audience. So we will need to cultivate a spirit of innovation through on-the-ground journalism that reestablishes the bonds of social trust between news media and consumers. Additionally, convincing Americans to change their minds about the facts will require a serious shift toward grassroots efforts to train them on how to responsibly navigate social media. To do this effectively, we must use social media to capitalize on human nature, which causes us to trust what our friends say more than what strangers say. Otherwise, the misinformation age will simply continue to serve as a driving force of our polarized culture.

This is a job for bridge builders – because the chasm between Americans and the truth can only be addressed by restoring people's connection to authentic news and information. Despite the swirling and powerful forces of falsehoods, bridge builders operating in journalism and social media do not accept the misinformation age as inevitable.

In this part, I'll tell the stories of bridge builders who believe that polarized people are often receptive to an alternative method of fact-checking that helps them reconnect with the truth. I'll introduce you to people who are reestablishing trust between journalists and the public, despite the breakdown in those ties in recent years. And I'll chronicle the experiences of bridge builders who believe that even social media, as polarized as it is, can be used to promote connection and understanding across cultures.

4

From Fiction to Fact

COVID-19 was genetically manipulated. Hospitals are being paid to inflate their fatality numbers. Hydroxychloroquine is an effective treatment for the novel coronavirus. Wearing a mask will make you more likely to get the disease. People who have received the flu vaccine have been injected with harmful coronaviruses.

All those claims are false. But they were nonetheless featured prominently in a 26-minute film, *Plandemic: The Hidden Agenda Behind COVID-19*, in spring 2020. The video, made by a California production company, was dubiously billed as a documentary when it began careening around the internet in the early months of the COVID-19 pandemic.[1] The video emerged at a time when countless Americans were desperately searching for answers as the coronavirus swept through the country, destroying lives and wrecking the economy. It got more than 9 million views on YouTube and more than 16 million reactions on Facebook. At one point, it was also trending on Twitter. Eventually, the social media platforms took it down – but not until the false claims featured in the video had entered the consciousness of people who viewed it and shared it.[2]

In many cases, conspiracy theories like those featured in *Plandemic* appeared to be designed to leverage the COVID-19 crisis to further divide Americans who were already split along typically polarized fault lines. For example, people who believe in QAnon, a wide-ranging extremist ideology promoted by conspiracists, circulated the debunked claim that the virus was intentionally released to hurt President Donald Trump's reelection chances or to control the population. Some radicalized conspiracists promoting QAnon bogusly described the coronavirus as a weapon designed by an evil cabal of liberals, while others, emboldened by nationalism, called it the "China virus" or the "Wuhan virus" because it originated in the country's city of Wuhan.[3] Although many of QAnon's false claims started on far-right website 4chan and made their way to other right-wing message boards, including some linked to White supremacist terrorism, they eventually jumped to mainstream social media, including Facebook and Twitter.[4]

Misinformation became seemingly unstoppable during the pandemic, despite repeated pledges of the mainstream social media companies to prevent blatant falsehoods from flourishing. The tech giants had previously vowed to expunge such harmful content, even as they continued to profit from mountains of questionable, if not altogether made-up, stories, photos, videos, memes, and posts that continued to find a happy home on their respective platforms, attracting attention and racking up advertising dollars. Social media algorithms – such as the ones that drive the Facebook News Feed and Twitter's main channel of tweets – deliver a mathematically curated flow of content based on what each individual user has liked, clicked on, shared, or retweeted in the past, as well as the content with which each user's digital friends have engaged. The upshot is that, during the worst moments of the pandemic, social media continued to serve as kindling for the raging flames of misinformation, further fueling our crisis of polarization.

"The internet has become an agent that makes people more and more extreme," said Sam Wineburg, founder

of the Stanford History Education Group and an expert
on teaching people how to trudge through digital lies.
Social media services use "machine learning to know
which content acts like Velcro that makes [it] impossible
to extricate ourselves."

Misinformation – that is, anything misleading or
untrue – and disinformation, a slight variant generally
defined as material deliberately designed to spread falsehoods, comprised a serious crisis long before *Plandemic*
began to spread and before QAnon was hatched.
During the 2016 presidential campaign, individual prof-
iteers capitalized on misinformation by distributing it
throughout the darkest corners of social media, while
Russia led a disinformation campaign designed to disrupt the election and propel Trump into the White
House.[5]

Those events were serious enough on their own to
call our collective attention to the broader crisis of falsehoods circulating online. But the coronavirus pandemic
rocketed the misinformation age into a dangerous new
stratosphere. It marked the first widespread example of
how misinformation not only can mislead and divide but
can even be fatal. People who failed to heed the advice
of public health officials to wear masks, practice social
distancing, and resist unproven medical treatments put
their lives and the lives of others at risk. On the whole,
Republicans were more likely than Democrats to spurn
masks and social distancing.[6]

Several studies showed that conservative news outlets
and commentators played a key role in spreading misleading reports about the pandemic, causing widespread
confusion and misunderstanding about the seriousness
of the crisis and what to do about it. "Taken together,
they paint a picture of a media ecosystem that ampli-
fies misinformation, entertains conspiracy theories, and
discourages audiences from taking concrete steps to
protect themselves and others," the *Washington Post*

summarized. One of the studies even noted that "infection and mortality rates are higher in places where one
pundit who initially downplayed the severity of the
pandemic – Fox News's Sean Hannity – reaches the
largest audiences."[7]

It certainly didn't help that Americans are not well
equipped educationally to navigate dynamic stories
involving complex scientific issues. This was a task
that most Americans once relied on mainstream media
to do for them. But the mainstream media have lost
their tight grip on the news cycle, leaving many people
to fend for themselves in the digital wild. The World
Health Organization labeled the collision of the pandemic and misinformation as an "infodemic" due to
the "over-abundance of information – some accurate
and some not – that makes it hard for people to find
trustworthy sources and reliable guidance when they
need it."[8]

"When any major news story breaks, that is a time
that is fertile for misinformation," said Alan Miller,
founder and CEO of the News Literacy Project. "As
journalists or, in the case of the pandemic, scientists are
trying to scramble to keep up with the facts, the bad
actors, the trolls, the sock puppets, and the bots swoop
in to perpetuate conspiracy theories and hoaxes and
viral rumors to try to set the narrative. With a heightened level of anxiety and interest in the public, it's a
time when emotions are aroused – and that's when we
tend to be most vulnerable to misinformation. People
are very prone to not only consuming what's out there
but also sharing it."

The absence of clarity amid a natural degree of bitterness and frustration over the isolating nature of the
pandemic plunged many Americans deeper into their
polarized chambers, further weakening the bridges of
social trust between the media and the public and
between health authorities and the public. This, in fact,

is the type of outcome the agents of disinformation desire.

"It's people's misconception that they're trying to persuade us of a particular point of view," Wineburg said of foreign actors – principally but not exclusively from Russia – and domestic provocateurs who circulate disinformation to divide Americans. "The whole chapter and verse of disinformation is to create muddled thinking, to create a situation where we throw our hands up and say, 'We don't know what to believe.' That's exactly what they want.'"

But bridge builders refuse to accept the misinformation age as our permanent reality. They believe that they can help Americans reconnect with the truth by training them how to sort fact from fiction on their own and to serve as promoters of authentic information in their own digital communities. They believe that strong bridges along our information superhighway are essential to combatting the forces of polarization that threaten our democracy – and thus, these connectors must be reinforced or rebuilt to help people see past the weaponized content that will otherwise continue to destabilize the critical infrastructure of our democracy.

When Katy Byron left Snapchat in 2018 to join The Poynter Institute, a nonprofit that promotes journalism and trains journalists, the world had already begun to wake up to the need to do something about misinformation. Trump's election two years earlier – followed by extensive public discourse over the role platforms like Facebook played in amplifying bogus content that enabled him to win – brought the crisis into sharp relief. But the scattershot efforts of social media companies and journalists to serve the public with a huge helping of reactive, top-down fact-checking were not doing much to stem the tide. Rather, misinformation continued to flourish. For example, the *New York Times* confirmed more than 4,000 episodes of misinformation in 2018 alone, such as lies about a caravan of migrants in Mexico heading toward the US border and a flurry of "mislabeled images and unfounded rumors [that] were used to attack the credibility of the multiple women who accused" then-Supreme Court nominee Brett Kavanaugh of sexual assault.[9] Trump himself originated or amplified many of the lies.

While professional fact-checking efforts were and remain admirable in their aim, they were and are not able to stamp out misinformation in large part because of the scale and speed with which falsehoods spread. Researchers at Indiana University demonstrated that it takes an average of about 10–20 hours for professional fact-checking material to circulate on social media after the initial posting of false content.[10] By then, the damage has been done.

Barring a shift to artificial intelligence for fact-checking, a not-too-far-out technological possibility that poses all sorts of concerns on its own, or a policy change by social media companies to systematically wipe out misinformation on their platforms – which they have been loath to do for legal, political, and financial reasons – we'll need another avenue. That's where efforts like Byron's Poynter program, MediaWise, come in.

Formed in 2018, the project was launched to teach American teenagers how to sort fact from fiction – and how to help their friends do the same on social media and messaging apps. Byron, who served as a producer at CNN and CNBC before becoming managing editor of news at Snapchat, joined Poynter to become the founding editor and program manager of MediaWise with a $3 million grant from Google's charitable arm, Google.org. In 2020, the group expanded its mission to include training older Americans. MediaWise set out to help people aged 50 and up learn the basic principles of fact-checking so that they can do it themselves, under the premise that we can't wait for professionals to do it for them. AARP, the powerful association of retirees, agreed to promote the program in its magazine, which reaches some 23 million Americans, and in emails to its members. And Facebook agreed to provide free advertising to help seniors who are active on its platform get training to improve their fact-validation skills.

"We want to empower people to find reliable and accurate information," Byron said when I spoke with her by video chat in the middle of the pandemic. "This work has never been more important than it is right now, in my view, because it has such a direct and immediate real-life impact on people's health, their wellbeing. People desperately need help improving their digital media literacy skills or establishing them in the first place."

We can't expect people to stop believing lies if we don't first equip them with the ability to identify them. After all, schools generally don't teach information validation as a skill. They're too busy prepping kids for standardized tests and college courses. But the work of helping Americans deal with misinformation is crucial to draining one of the main tanks that fuels our epidemic of divisiveness. Without such work, people will continue to be fooled and slip deeper into their polarized echo chambers.

"Pretty much for every single news story you see, there is misinformation that would appeal to either side of an issue," said Alex Mahadevan, program manager for MediaWise's seniors project. "Those who have already dug their heels in, they can share it with people who might be on the fence. The cutting and shifting of context in all this content we see online is providing this convenient narrative that helps drive a stake into the divide between both sides. So as we see more of this misinformation, it's just dividing the country even more."

Evidence of our widening crisis of disconnection is plainly visible underneath the posts on mainstream social media platforms like Facebook, YouTube, Instagram, and TikTok – not to mention conservative social networking services that blatantly refuse to remove falsehoods. "It's when you go to the comments that you see the discourse happening," said Alexa Volland, who manages MediaWise's network of teen fact-checkers. "You see one side presenting information that directly falls in line with their belief system, and then you have the other side commenting on information that makes them feel validated. It's in this drawn line in the sand where all the needed context seems to live."

Helping Americans walk along bridges of truth by sifting through digital chaos and delivering that needed context to their friends and family is the mission of groups like MediaWise and the News Literacy Project. Both started as services geared toward educating students about how to sort fact from fiction, but both have since branched out to help older Americans do the same. In a way, their collective mission is to equip people with the skills of traditional journalists, since our entire profession is based on confirming or disproving information and assessing the validity of sources. These are the basic abilities that everyday people now need to live their lives online.

MediaWise's curriculum is based on a simple set of fact-checking principles recommended by Wineburg's Stanford History Education Group, which devised the recommendations after reaching an empirical conclusion that professional fact-checkers are more proficient at sorting fact from fiction than historians.[11] The recommendations are derived from professional fact-checkers' habit of "lateral reading," which involves visiting other websites to assess the validity of sources. Many internet users, including highly educated types, simply check the "About Us" page, look to see if the site has a ".org" address, or use their general heuristics to make determinations based on the look and feel of the page. But those strategies are woefully insufficient, given how easily online content can be manipulated to look legitimate.

"People talk about, 'We just need critical thinking,' as if critical thinking is some elixir. No. First we need some basic skills," Wineburg said. "We need to teach people that the longer they stay on an unfamiliar webpage from an unfamiliar organization, the more they fall into the clutches of possible bad actors – and it is exactly the opposite of what professionals do. Professionals spend fractions of a second, when they land on an unfamiliar page, before going to the rest of the internet in order to get the bearings of that original page they landed on. It's a completely different paradigm."

Further exploration of the methods of professional fact-checkers led Wineburg to summarize them in three straightforward guidelines for MediaWise to instill in its trainees:

1. "Who's behind the information?"
2. "What is the evidence?"
3. "What do other sources say?"

"They're so classic but still so good," Byron said. "Those three questions can take you a long way, and it's very digestible for the public."

MediaWise also teaches its amateur fact-checkers – both teenagers and older people – to slow down before assessing the validity of information they consume and share on social media. "People don't want to read past the headline," Byron said. "[We're] trying to break that cycle of people's mindset of click, retweet, reshare. Think about what you're reading, what you're seeing. Do you want to share this with your network? Do you know if it's accurate? Is it real? It's a really hard habit to break."

Perhaps the most important question is whether Americans want to break that habit. Are they receptive at all to learning the fact-checking skills they need to restore their connection with the truth? If people don't care about the facts, what's the point?

The good news is that most people seem to understand that misinformation is bedeviling the country. About 67 percent of Americans say that "made-up" news and information "causes a great deal of confusion about the basic facts of current issues," while 24 percent say it creates "some confusion," and only 8 percent say it creates "not much" or no confusion at all, according to a survey conducted in early 2019 by the Pew Research Center.[12] "People are saying in large numbers now that they are not confident that they can actually sort fact from fiction or that they can't determine what's real news from fake news," said Miller of the News Literacy Project.

In Wineburg's assessment, there are two types of people. First, there's "the user who is so deeply entrenched in motivated reasoning or confirmation bias that no content or no fact check that they see is going to do anything to affect what they think." They are, as he said, "true believers" in whatever dosage of misinformation they ingest, whether it's QAnon, myths that vaccines are dangerous, or the so-called "birther conspiracy" that falsely claims former President Barack Obama was not born in the United States. "There's a lot of them," Wineburg said, referring to the fact disbelievers. But he believes the majority of Americans fit into a second group, which he calls "the searchers of goodwill."

"Those are the people who go to the internet with a genuine desire to know," he said. "It is that group who, if we teach some basic ways of ascertaining reliability, we hope we can bring them back into the fold of respecting facts and respecting verified knowledge."

It would behoove us to treat Americans with a degree of grace when it comes to their ability to sort fact from fiction. For starters, we don't teach it in schools, as noted earlier. Yes, we teach facts. But we do not teach how to assess facts – at least not very well. Which is why Wineburg advocates for the integration of fact-checking lessons within existing subjects in school. "Schools do not teach media literacy and they're not going to," he said. "Schools teach science, they teach math, they teach social studies, they teach civics." What we need, he said, is lessons in biology class on the safety of vaccines, lessons in history class on the lie of Holocaust denial, and lessons in math class on statistical manipulation.

That's precisely what the News Literacy Project is doing. As of the time of this writing, Miller's organization was on track to equip 20,000 educators with the experience to teach news literacy to 3 million middle school and high school students annually. One of the group's methods is a free virtual classroom tool called Checkology, which is particularly well suited for the kind of remote learning that became common during the pandemic.[13]

"We believe that news literacy is an essential skill in the information age," Miller said. "It's really a survival skill. We live in what should be a digital golden age with more credible information available to us literally at our fingertips than ever before, but it's being overwhelmed by a tsunami of misinformation that doesn't seek to inform us in a dispassionate, accurate, contextual way, but seeks to persuade us, to sell to us, to misinform us, or to exploit us."

Integrating coursework on fact-checking into the core curriculum of America's schools is perhaps the best way to combat the misinformation age in the long run. But even if we start today, it will take generations to have a significant effect. An education revolution won't help America's older people, which is why MediaWise and the News Literacy Project hope to reach them by training them to fact-check on their own.

MediaWise's volunteer trainers don't "begin with the mindset that these people don't know what they're doing and they're all bigots who are going to be dug in and not listening," Mahadevan said. Instead, they begin webinars and, once the pandemic is over, will begin in-person training sessions by talking to seniors about the need to root out nonpolitical misinformation, such as online scams. That's something everyone can agree on. Then the trainers discuss the dangers of misinformation about health, including but not exclusive to bogus coronavirus cures. "Talking about scams and health misinformation before jumping right into political stuff [helps] us with this demographic," Mahadevan said.

The trainers also provide basic information to seniors on how social media works. Many people don't realize that social media companies employ algorithms that curate the information they do and do not see in their feeds.[14] "So we're constantly being fed things that the algorithms and the programs and the companies know that we want to see, and we encourage people to get out of their own echo chamber," said Heaven Taylor-Wynn, who manages social media content for MediaWise.

Another key to ensuring that people accept the legitimacy of fact-checking work is transparency: simply displaying the process through which the fact-checker ascertained the validity of the source material. "It's show, not just tell," said Kristyn Wellesley, editorial director of MediaWise. MediaWise fact-checkers "show you exactly where they found the information, and they will walk you through it. That is so unique to what we do. We're not just telling you these tips. We will actually show you how to do it."

Professional journalists also need to be more transparent about their processes to rebuild the public's trust in the legitimacy of professionally produced news, said Miller, a former *Los Angeles Times* reporter. "We as a business did not do a good job of explaining to the public what we did and how we did it and why," he said. "I think it really left us vulnerable to a combination of attacks from the right, from the left, from online media sources, and some self-inflicted wounds." Instead of remaining secretive about how we discern the facts, journalists need to be open about it, "demystifying the news gathering process, the vetting, the accountability, the transparency that at least aspirationally is reflected in quality journalism," Miller said.

The teenage fact-checkers for MediaWise understand that, on the internet, transparency breeds trust. As part of the program, they fact-check conspiracy theories through the creation of YouTube videos, Instagram stories, and TikTok clips, outlining precisely how they assessed the veracity of the claims. That meticulous process allows them to debunk harmful information before it has a chance to rapidly wind its way through a viral pathway. Ironically, it also capitalizes on the same algorithmic potential that empowers falsehoods: since we're more likely to see and trust content in our feeds from our friends and family, then it's best for fact-checking material to be posted by them, instead of professional news organizations.

During the pandemic, MediaWise fact-checking efforts covered a wide range of angles:

> "Are Chinese hospitals refusing to treat patients to reduce new COVID-19 case numbers?"
> "Does vaping protect you from COVID-19?"
> "Did Chinese doctors confirm African people are immune to the coronavirus?"
> "Are these blacklight images of bacteria on hands legit?"
> "Can children transmit the coronavirus?"

All of those questions were fact-checked by teenagers through the creation of TikTok videos. (Answers, in order: likely false, although China was believed to be falsifying numbers in other ways. No. "Not legit." "Needs context." Yes.)[15]

"Our teen fact-checkers will take that viral claim, they will research it, and they will show you step by step how they looked into it, giving it all that necessary context," Volland said. "It's showing and being transparent and making fact-checking as easy and accessible as possible – and that goes across all age ranges. Honestly, if a teen can do it, then anyone can do it."

⊱✦✦✦⊰

Despite the best efforts of news literacy trainers to give Americans the tools they need to navigate the misinformation age, it will all be for naught if we don't experience a cultural shift of sorts. That is, we must collectively recognize that misinformation poses a serious danger to our democracy and, as the pandemic has showed us, to our health. And each of us must help our friends and family – that is, the people we care about the most – avoid falling prey to lies. This is especially critical given how threats like QAnon are not just dividing us politically – they're entrapping countless people in a vortex of fear and tearing apart families.[16] If these threats are allowed to fester, our fissures will intensify as we fail to reconnect with the truth, making bridge building nearly impossible.

Ironically, reverse engineering the social media platforms to capitalize on the connective tissue they've formed between like-minded people would help limit the flow of misinformation. That is, we already know that social media shows us the content our friends and family think is most interesting. So if we can cultivate a culture of personal fact-checking on social media, then we can leverage the power of responsible personal relationships to change hearts and minds – because then, due to the way it's designed, social media will begin spreading facts to our friends and family, instead of fiction.

Top-down fact-checking efforts by professional news organizations are admirable and needed – but they're not usually going to make people see the light because we are often impervious to the truth when it's delivered by people who aren't part of our preferred social groups. But when the facts are dished out by people who are close to us, we will become more receptive to the truth and we will become less polarized. All it requires is a few dedicated insiders to take action to help disrupt the flow of misinformation that otherwise threatens to radicalize members of the group. This is why the models employed by MediaWise and the News Literacy Project are so important: because they teach people to fish in the form of training them how to fact-check, instead of feeding them professionally composed fact-checking content at a time when Americans often don't trust the media.

"I think that most people probably are not knowingly and wittingly sharing misinformation that could be damaging to the country's civic life or public health. They're sharing this with their friends and family, so why would you want to [hurt] them?" Miller said. "What really is critical here is that we create a new public ethos around the news and information that we consume, and we share [that information] with an enhanced sense of personal responsibility."

It can be done. Think about it as akin to successful public service campaigns over the years. Americans need to absorb the attitude that "misinformation stops with me," much like Smokey Bear taught us that "only you can prevent forest fires," and we must all absorb the attitude that "friends don't let friends share misinformation," much like we've been taught that friends don't let friends drink and drive, Miller said. "We need a sea change in public attitudes and behaviors, like we've seen around issues such as smoking and drunk driving and littering, with enhanced mindfulness so that people realize they can either be part of the misinformation problem or part of an information solution, and that only the public – really, all of us – can prevent us from sliding into an information dystopia, where I fear we may be headed."

In summer 2020 – in the midst of the pandemic – Miller was trying to figure out how to best communicate the need for a cultural shift to treat misinformation as a public health crisis. That's when he came up with the idea to tweak illustrator Walt Kelly's famous 1970s "Pogo" cartoon showing the eponymous character staring at a pile of garbage in a forest. "We have met the enemy and he is us," Pogo says in the original cartoon, which raised awareness about littering and pollution.[17] Miller had his team at the News Literacy Project compose a new version of the cartoon. Instead of garbage, Pogo is now staring at social media logos and symbols, such as the "like" button, littering the landscape.[18]

"This is a different kind of pollution, but once again the enemy is us," Miller said. "People tend to believe it's either the people creating it – the extremists, the conspiracy theorists, or the Russians – or it's the social media platforms that are permitting it on the platform, all of which are true. But it can't get the virality it gets without all of us spreading it."

5

From Caricature to Nuance

They're hillbillies.
They're unemployed coal miners.
They're uneducated.
They're religious wackos.
They're conservative wingnuts.

The harsh stereotypes of the people of Appalachia are deeply entrenched in the American consciousness. During the 2016 presidential campaign, those ugly caricatures flooded the airwaves, newspapers, websites, and social media accounts of powerful news outlets responsible for accurately depicting the people of a sprawling region that ranges from portions of southwest New York state southward through Pennsylvania, Kentucky, West Virginia, Tennessee, and into parts of Georgia and Alabama.

"Welcome to Trump County, USA," *Vanity Fair* blared in a headline on a story reported from Monongalia County, West Virginia. The writer led the story with a lurid anecdote: "It is a little after midnight on a Friday in late January. I am in a strip club in Morgantown, West Virginia, drinking shit American beer that tastes like ice and newspaper. A man is passing me a semi-automatic handgun and telling me to pull the trigger," the story begins.[1] "I am in West Virginia to understand

Donald Trump," the writer explains later in the story. "At least, to the extent that the political embodiment of a Hardee's commercial needs to be understood. Specifically, I'm here to understand the people who want him to be president."

Another harsh headline before the election, from the *New York Post*, promised can't-miss insight: "Why 'White Trash' Americans Are Flocking to Donald Trump."[2]

A photo gallery from the *Guardian* painted a narrow portrait of people in the region: "Life in Appalachia: Walmart, Church, Politics, and a Tight Community."[3]

As the exploitative coverage reached coastal elites, it was evident in Morgantown that the portrayal of Appalachia was deepening the divide between locals and outsiders. At West Virginia University (WVU), journalism professor Dana Coester was fed up. "At one point, I had a PowerPoint slide of all the headlines from 'Trump Country,' 'Trump Nation,'" Coester told me when I visited the WVU Reed College of Media's state-of-the-art multimedia journalism center in Morgantown. "It was the *Atlantic*, the *New Yorker* – everybody had done their stint in West Virginia or Appalachia. We started to joke that there aren't even that many miners left, but all of them had been interviewed by national media to be representative of the region."

Albeit with some notable exceptions, the coverage had a generally acidic tone, highlighting extremes and regurgitating tired stereotypes. For Coester's journalism professor colleague Gina Dahlia, it was hurtful. The typical story highlighted "the redneck that was drilling a hole in the side of the truck and putting the Confederate flag in it," said Dahlia, her searing eyes exuding the pain of someone whose reputation had been dragged through the mud.

She was not surprised. "I was born and raised in West Virginia, so I've been here my entire life," she said. "So

I've definitely seen media swooping in." She recalled TV journalist Geraldo Rivera descending upon West Virginia to cover the Sago Mine disaster of 2006. "He was trying to interview exactly the stereotypical West Virginian. It didn't matter if there were educated people standing around. He wanted the toothless, coal-mining wife to interview," she said. "That was just one example of what I've seen living here my entire life."

So when Trump's victory turned the world's gaze toward the nearly defunct US coal-mining industry and pockets of rural poverty, the media's emphasis on Appalachia's extremes intensified. Numerous outlets dispatched correspondents to the region to puzzle out how Trump had prevailed – ignoring the fact that polls showed the extent to which educated, wealthy, suburban voters had played a crucial role in hoisting Trump into the White House.[4]

"Our phone rang off the hook after the 2016 election," said Tim Marema, vice president of the Kentucky-based Center for Rural Strategies and editor of the nonprofit's *Daily Yonder*, a rural news publication. "It's not hard to tell which journalists already had their story before they called and were only looking for information and sources that confirmed their preconceived opinion, which is literally the definition of prejudice. Some people talked to us like we were a casting agency: 'I'm looking for a coal miner who voted for Trump.'"[5]

The stories and broadcasts were simply "reinforcing some kind of Trump narrative" outlined by editors in far-off coastal newsrooms, Coester said. "We had so many earnest people coming in. It was embarrassing for them. It was embarrassing for us."

To be sure, some outlets pieced together packages of coverage providing nuanced perspectives on the region. Marema specifically noted the *New York Times*, the *Washington Post*, and NBC News for their "very thoughtful and even-handed" coverage. But many reporters simply exploited locals who voted for Trump, worsening the disconnect between journalists and the public at a time when trust in the news media was already suffering.

The assignments took similar shape: "Go find someone on food stamps who voted for Trump" or "Go find someone on disability or Medicare who voted for Trump," Marema said in an email interview. "There was a degree of empathy in these stories for difficult conditions some Americans face. But that was lost within the paternalism and self-righteousness."

In the months leading up to the election, Coester and WVU visiting journalism professor Nancy Andrews had begun researching and preparing a proposal for a news project to provide better coverage of the region. But they still didn't know exactly what they wanted it to be. The day after the election, however, they sprang into action. (Full disclosure: Andrews was one of my editors during my tenure as a reporter for the *Detroit Free Press* from 2012 to 2015.)

"It's actually kind of funny because we had pages and pages of reports and planning and meetings," Coester said. The day after the election, they set the plan aside. "We wrote this one-paragraph mission statement. And then we just got started."

The initial concept was simple: launch a "pop-up publication" to blanket Appalachia with comprehensive news stories and multimedia coverage during the first 100 days of the Trump administration.

Within weeks, the leaders formed a collaboration between the WVU Reed College of Media, West Virginia Public Broadcasting, and the *Daily Yonder* to tell authentic stories with the hope of rebuilding trust, forming new connections, and bringing attention to the region's multiplicity of issues. They named the project *100 Days in Appalachia*, aiming to make a national impact with coverage of the region: "Our feeling was if we can surface a more complex narrative about this region, then we're training an audience how to look with more complexity at whatever community they're reading about, not just their own," Coester said.

As a native of West Virginia, Dahlia couldn't pass up the chance to help lead the project. "I definitely felt a personal interest in trying to change that narrative because I'm so tired of people assuming that we're not as good as them, that we're not as smart as them, that we're not as educated as them," she said.

From the beginning, the goal of *100 Days in Appalachia* was to use journalists embedded in local communities to highlight the region's challenges and opportunities, failures and victories, insularity and diversity. In doing so, the editors envisioned forming partnerships with for-profit and nonprofit news outlets, enabling those organizations to publish locally generated stories on a broader platform. "The whole vision for this was to create a regional publication that was actually talking to national media – and to external, national audiences – to say, 'Whatever you think you know about the region, you're probably wrong,'" Coester said. "We wanted to create a very assertive counternarrative, which also had the goal of trying to restore some faith in coverage. I mean, there is a very legitimate reason why people do not have trust in media coverage and representation of themselves."

Andrews saw this first hand. The multimedia editor and photographer led the online publication's initial feature, "100 Days, 100 Voices," a series designed to authentically depict the people and places of the region through photography. She resolved not to fall into the trap of lazily training her camera lens on blighted communities and seeking out only explicit images of poverty. Instead, she sought to deliver a kaleidoscopic view of Appalachian schools, churches, businesses, and residents, without ignoring the region's problems, but also without exploiting them.

"We tend to think of stereotypes very much in visual terms. I've joked that when a photographer comes to Appalachia, the color is somehow drained out of their camera," Andrews said with a knowing laugh.

"We're all black and white and dirt," Dahlia added.

There's a reason for it. "Because it fit the narrative," Andrews said. "So one of my basic rules was that I would always publish in color. No matter how monochrome the scene looked, Appalachia is in full color."

As the veteran multimedia journalist ventured into Appalachian communities, she began hearing story after story of disenfranchised locals who felt misrepresented and mistreated by the national media.

At one point, her project took her to a church in McDowell County. "McDowell County is one of the poorest counties – it's often the poster child for different issues. It's a place on politicians' punch list," Andrews said. Rather than rundown and rickety, she said, the church had spotless carpeting, beautiful oak floors, and bright-red curtains. When she was sizing it up for photo opportunities, a parishioner came up to her, held her hand, and looked into her eyes. "Please, please be kind to us," the church member told her.

"And I knew what she meant," Andrews said. "She went on to tell a story about her experience with media and how the extreme was shown and how they went and photographed the snake handlers" – an isolated Christian sect that sometimes integrates venomous snakes into its spiritual practices.[6] The West Virginian churchgoer wasn't protesting the fact that the media had featured snake handlers in the past, but she objected to those images reflecting "the only representation" of her community – "that extreme view of religion," Andrews said.

When news coverage capitalizes on extremes for the sake of web traffic or ratings, it widens the divide between journalists and the communities they cover.

"It's really poignant to people," Andrews said. "That's where that lack of trust" originates.

The "100 Days, 100 Voices" project "set the tone for the publication," reflecting a degree of diversity that doesn't make its way into the national narrative about the region, Marema said. "We see people worshiping and laying on hands in the Christian tradition, which is the way I came up. We see immigrants from different faiths. We see some small business owners, farmers, some hipsters, kids, civil rights advocates, Trump supporters, a high school band, a blues musician. It challenges my own notions about who lives in Appalachia, while at the same time reaffirming my own little cultural niche." He added: "That's what '100 Days' has done overall – elevated hundreds of voices who together give you a larger vision of Appalachia. There is no singular Appalachia. . . . Within those unique details, there are patterns that help us see a bigger picture without succumbing to stereotypes."

That type of coverage is increasingly difficult to find because local news outlets, which know their communities the best, have been crushed by the decline of print advertising revenue and paid subscriptions. Their demise has national consequences. In the absence of trusted local outlets – which thrived on relationships between journalists and the community – the attention of news consumers has shifted toward national outlets and often extremely partisan online communities that foster polarization through social media. Plus, the news industry's pivot toward emphasizing reader metrics to maximize revenue has unfortunately led to more sensational headlines and less intricacy in many quarters. Consequently, readers and viewers have grown increasingly cynical about the news content they encounter.

About six in ten Americans "think news organizations do not understand people like them," according to a Pew Research Center poll conducted from February through March 2020. That includes 61 percent of White people, 58 percent of Black people, and 55 percent of Hispanic people. Overall, 39 percent of White Americans say that it is their political views that are most misunderstood by the media; 34 percent of Black people cite their "personal characteristics" as being the least understood; and 26 percent of Hispanic people say that it is their "personal interests" that are most misunderstood.[7]

"It's not an Appalachia problem. It's a universal journalism problem that so many communities feel not well represented almost anywhere you go," Coester said. "I'm not certain a local journalist can do the labor of fixing that, but it's probably the first place to start."

Andrews rejected the suggestion that journalists can't go beyond their predilection for stories rooted in conflict. But she acknowledged that the business model of for-profit journalism is weighted toward anything that generates an eye-popping headline. What's more, most traditional news outlets – with the exception of a chosen few that can charge for online subscriptions, such as the *Times* and the *Post* – are bleeding cash. Consequently, their journalism too often takes the easy route.

"The cheapest type of journalism to do is reaction journalism. It's, 'Who's winning today? What did so-and-so say today?'" Andrews said.

Making matters worse, the news cycle moves so fast that there's insufficient payback for many for-profit journalism outlets to pursue in-depth stories packed full of nuance and solutions. But nonprofit outlets like *100 Days in Appalachia* are serving readers, not shareholders. That gives them the flexibility to pursue stories that others might ignore.

⁎⁎⁎⁎⁎

To reestablish trust between journalists and the public – that is, to build bridges between them – requires rethinking the way journalism is carried out. Which is one key reason why *100 Days in Appalachia* quickly ditched its temporary status. The organization's leaders decided 100 days wasn't enough. There were too many stories that would go untold if they limited themselves to that period of time. To keep the project going, Coester secured funding from foundation donors in addition to ongoing support from WVU.[8]

With sufficient funding to continue beyond their initial period, the leaders transitioned the upstart project into a venture with an indefinite horizon and additional partnerships with local and major media outlets. "We quickly realized . . . that our issues have now become America's issues, and there was no way we could stop the conversation after 100 days because these issues were not going away," Dahlia said.

From the beginning, the *100 Days in Appalachia* crew sought to highlight the voices and faces of Appalachian residents who have been largely ignored in the popular press. The publication launched a 360-degree video series called, "Muslim in Appalachia," to illustrate how the region is not religiously monolithic.[9]

"Yes, I do wear a headscarf on my head, and I probably don't look like your stereotypical American," West Virginia resident Sara Berzingi, a Kurdish American Muslim whose family moved to America when she was 4 years old, said in one of the videos. "Our nation is so great and so powerful because we're all from so many different backgrounds."[10]

In one story, Brian Gardner, a student who "defines himself as a biracial, LGBT, religious minority," is featured joining hundreds of West Virginians protesting Trump's ban on people from certain Muslim-majority countries from visiting the United States.[11]

Another compelling story featured the first dance in West Virginia state history for LGBTQ youth. Students from at least 10 counties attended, including a 15-year-old gay boy interviewed by the West Virginia Public Broadcasting journalist who wrote the story for *100 Days in Appalachia*. "I've never actually been to a dance with others before – like a big dance like this. And I'm kinda nervous that I'm going to embarrass myself," the student said. "There's that little anxiety that's pushing up against me. But it's gonna go away."[12]

What these stories demonstrate is that we, as journalists, can be bridge builders. We can use our platform to paint authentic portraits of people and their communities, fostering trust and understanding with readers and viewers. Those seeds of trust help combat the tendency among some consumers – conservatives in particular – to dismiss legitimate journalism as "fake news" when the coverage makes them uncomfortable.

"When people see themselves and hear themselves, there's an incredible validation and resonance there," Coester said. "People understand that journalists are going to write about problems, but to do so authentically and also with that nuance [is important] because people are smart, and they'll see if you're just sensationalizing an issue or their identity."

The complex and layered nature of the coverage, images, and videos published by *100 Days in Appalachia* strikes a balanced tone that naturally generates trust. "Things are not two-sided. They're multifaceted," Andrews said. "It's almost like there's this orchestra of events happening out there, and if we're always playing the same note, (a) that's boring and you tune out, but (b) you don't get the whole song. You don't get the whole orchestra."

The journalists' goal is not to deny the reality that West Virginians, as a whole, have conservative political tendencies, but instead to punch holes in the one-track national narrative. "We understand those challenges because we're one of those states where every county voted for Trump," Dahlia said. "So we get that. But it wasn't every person in every county."

West Virginia's political composition, in fact, is much more complicated. "The media cannot untether itself from binary political coverage," Coester said. "And if there's anything that West Virginia voters tell us, it's how fluid people are in their relationship to politics."

In a binary paradigm, there's no room for nuance. For example, when West Virginia teachers went on strike for better compensation in 2018, the national narrative cast the story as a "progressive uprising" against Trump, according to Coester's characterization. In contrast, a *100 Days in Appalachia* story that was picked up by national news outlet Salon showed how the strike had nothing to do with Trump. It stemmed from opposition to low compensation for teachers.[13] Two years later, of course, Trump won West Virginia again in a landslide in the general election.

"We've got a lot of women who are picketing for the first time in their lives, who are taking a social action about something that matters in their community, who voted for Trump, and still support Trump," Coester said. "That didn't mean it wasn't a worthwhile story. It just wasn't a Trump-centric story."

The upshot is that journalists can be bridge builders without compromising their principles of objectivity and truth. "Journalism can bring communities together," Andrews said. "Throughout history we have gathered around the campfire to tell a story. So we need story-tellers. Sometimes they're investigative storytellers, and sometimes it's just how we tell stories so that we get to know each other and know our community. That's how you know your neighbor. Some of those stories just bring you to tears and make you love your neighbor a little bit more."

100 Days in Appalachia's deft handling of these sto-ries illustrates the importance of maintaining vibrant

local journalism organizations despite the economic
challenges they face. "It's really easy when you're covering a region to paint people who live there with a
broad brush, but *100 Days in Appalachia* worked really
hard to take a more nuanced approach and highlight
the diversity of the people who live there," said Joseph
Lichterman, senior business associate at The Lenfest
Institute, which studies journalism's evolving role in
democracy. "They're complicating the story in a really
good way and a way that makes you think about the
reality on the ground more intelligently. They're on the
ground there and know the communities really well and
aren't parachuting in to discover what this is all about."

The *100 Days in Appalachia* leaders made the case
that the national media fundamentally misunderstand
people in middle America in part because they often
do not have an established local presence. "What ends
up happening is somebody flies in from New York and
there's no trust and there's no connection. So they're
not getting the same type of nuance that we would be,"
Dahlia said. "They always come in and feel like they
know us. They come in with this preconceived notion."

Certainly there are exceptions. Many national journalists let the story come to them, not the other way
around. I'd like to think of myself as one of them. Then
again, after I visited the headquarters of *100 Days in
Appalachia* in Morgantown, I had to fight the urge to
frame this chapter around the aging smokestack I saw
in the distance through the high-rise window of the publication's gleaming newsroom. That dissonant imagery
resonated for me because of its roots in the stereotypical
portrait of Appalachia. But I realized, upon interviewing the publication's editors, that my instincts were
precisely the problem. The bottom line is that national
journalists like me are often not well suited to tell local
stories authentically. (Though I certainly hope I've done
so in this chapter.) By and large, local journalists should

be handling local journalism – but that likely requires investing in nonprofit journalism, since most national media outlets have decided it's not profitable to keep reporters embedded in local communities in the long run.

Local journalists can and should be trusted to tell stories about their communities truthfully on a regular basis. "There's an expectation that if you are of a region, that somehow you won't be authentic to the region – that somehow we would look at it as a PR moment," Coester said. "I mean, we're journalists. We know how to practice good journalism."

Covering complex stories authentically requires executing a boots-on-the-ground strategy that doesn't come easy. *100 Days in Appalachia* shares a digital managing editor with West Virginia Public Broadcasting and gets reporting help from several classes of students at the journalism school. It has also assembled a network of part-time professional editors throughout the region and cultivated local freelance writers and photographers.

"One of the things we were worried about was, 'Oh, my gosh, how are we going to get quality content?'" Coester said. "But there was such a hunger in the region for an outlet to tell other stories that we became the go-to place for a lot of people across the region."

The publication's nonprofit funders have enabled the journalists to continue focusing on coverage of complex matters that doesn't necessarily go viral on social media but instead generates genuine conversation about serious issues facing the people of Appalachia. That's in sharp contrast to the type of headlines aimed at provoking comments, replies, likes, reactions, and shares on Facebook and Twitter, which generally reward content that spawns emotional reactions instead of contemplative responses. "Funding from other sources has helped us be more complex than what the market wants to support," Coester said.

The group's embrace of collaborative journalism has also made this possible. Collaborative journalism is a movement in the news industry that calls for different outlets to work together instead of remaining isolated for competitive reasons. Bridge builders recognize that, to reach the public, they often need to first build bridges among themselves.

It's a tough concept for many journalists to embrace because of their deep-seated desire to generate scoops. We love to be first – and to get credit for it. And we're often under pressure from our editors to deliver exclusives. But the economic reality of journalism in the digital age requires a new mentality.

At first, some potential publishing partners were skeptical of the collaborative model proposed by the *100 Days in Appalachia* editors. But the quality of the site's journalism and the editors' openness to sharing stories paved the way for collaboration. *100 Days in Appalachia* has developed content-sharing partnerships with dozens of news organizations, including local outlets like *Your Voice Ohio*, Cleveland-based *Belt Magazine*, Pittsburgh's *PublicSource*, Alabama's *AL.com*, Atlanta-based *Bitter Southerner*, and North Carolina-based *Scalawag*. With their forces combined, the *100 Days in Appalachia* network has attracted attention from national and international outlets and now co-publishes content in, for example, the *Guardian*.

"To us, that's an extraordinary success because now we're making sure that narratives from the region that might not have seen any eyeballs outside of the region are" getting international attention, Coester said. Outlets that previously didn't have the resources to reach audiences throughout and beyond Appalachia suddenly have a partner to help them make a bigger impact. "So we can benefit each other and grow our audience on both ends," Coester said.

Collaboration marks a sharp departure from journalism of the past. "Competition used to be the news model that was supposed to deliver the best content," said Marema, collaborator on *100 Days in Appalachia*. Earlier in his career, he spent time at daily newspapers in North Carolina that competed intensely with other outlets. "There was a remote chance we might collaborate on a troublesome public-documents request or an open-meeting problem. But the rest was competition," he said.

But many newspapers in North Carolina, like elsewhere, have since plummeted. Reporters, editors, budgets, and editions have been slashed. "No one can afford to compete that way now. So we need a different model if we are going to feed democracy what it eats, which is ideas and information," Marema said. Collaboration, he said, serves that purpose. That's why the *Daily Yonder* and the Center for Rural Strategies "pursue a course of collaboration and partnership by default," including with *100 Days in Appalachia*. "What matters the most to us isn't that we are the ones who carry quality information about rural America – it's that quality information about rural America reaches the largest audience possible," Marema said. "Partnerships can help you do that in a sustainable way."

For struggling newspapers and digital journalism operations, partnering with nonprofit sites can help ensure that their coverage is well-rounded without devoting precious resources to stories that would inevitably involve reporters parachuting into communities for short periods that culminate in questionable snapshots of local issues. But it requires for-profit news organizations to acknowledge their deficiencies, said Andrews, whose past experience as a journalist at the *Washington Post* and the *Detroit Free Press* gives her insight from both ends of the spectrum. "Those who choose to partner realize that the added value is the local expertise," she said. "For some people, when they're maybe too big, they don't want to cede that they don't have an expertise. So you have to be willing to say somebody can bring something to you."

For journalism partnerships to be successful, it requires the cultivation of relationships, idea-sharing, and frequent communication across newsrooms. At *100 Days in Appalachia*, journalists throughout the network have exchanged story concepts and planned projects together. "We use their stuff, they use ours, as we each deem appropriate," Marema said. "That's one level of cooperation. I think the deeper level is more about sharing our perspective about our patch of Appalachia, which helps extend the reach and content to other parts of the region. We've also shared sources, data, research, and story ideas."

100 Days in Appalachia has focused much of its collaborative coverage on potential solutions to the region's various crises, including poverty, opioids, and a lack of economic opportunity. That emphasis on solution fits with a growing recognition that journalism must seek to provide answers, not just expose problems. That, too, stands in contrast to the industry's long-running obsession with focusing on conflict and snubbing problem-solving.

But building bridges requires pursuing solutions – a process that demonstrates commitment to community – not just dwelling on problems. "Appalachia's problems are complicated, and you almost can't enter reporting about them without it being solutions-oriented," Coester said.

It's admittedly difficult to pull off. After all, it's much simpler to sit at your desk in a newsroom and write stories based on what's trending on Google or Twitter, which will inevitably generate hits.

"Solutions journalism is much harder; it's resource-intensive, community-building reporting," Coester said. "And I think we have a long way to go as an industry to make that a part of the bread and butter of reporting instead of the exception. It's resource-intensive and it's relationship-intensive."

Lichterman, who studied *100 Days in Appalachia* for a weekly newsletter on solutions-oriented journalism, said the movement builds trust between readers and journalists. "You aren't just writing about what's wrong," he said. Rather, "you're reframing the journalistic lens" to show how hurdles can be surmounted.

***

Readers, it turns out, welcome a pivot toward solutions-oriented journalism. Beginning in 2018, the *Milwaukee Journal Sentinel* abandoned most opinion stories and editorials in favor of journalism focused on solutions. (Gannett Co., which owns my employer, *USA Today*, also owns the *Journal Sentinel*.) Gone are political screeds and hot-take columns aimed at stirring outrage or blasting one politician or another.

Instead, the publication began reporting on issues like bystander intervention programs aimed at reducing violence on college campuses, the role of deindustrialization in undermining Milwaukee neighborhoods, and how bike lanes can make streets safer for bicyclists and motorists alike. When the US Supreme Court took up a case on gerrymandering, the *Journal Sentinel* highlighted a nonpartisan solution instead of publishing divisive columns blaming one side or the other.[14]

Web traffic figures have spiked for the *Journal Sentinel*, and complaints have plummeted. In the first three months of 2019, page views per story doubled, compared with the same period a year earlier. In short, readers liked what they saw.[15]

Why? David Haynes, editorial page editor of the *Journal Sentinel* and inaugural editor of the publication's "Ideas Lab," believes that commentary has been "cheapened" with the flood of opinions on the air and on social media. "The sheer volume of this white-hot commentary makes it difficult for thoughtful opinion writing to break through," he wrote for the American Press Institute. "I also suspect some readers are worn out after the nonstop viciousness of partisan politics, which has only been magnified in the Trump era."[16]

While for-profit outlets are perhaps best positioned to make the biggest impact, nonprofits are especially well suited to reimagine the practice of journalism. Andrews believes journalism as an institution has failed to properly engage community members because of the fundamental principles that have sustained journalism for decades. For example, journalists are typically prohibited from serving in public institutions or publicly sharing their opinions on anything except mundane topics like sports, food, and pop culture.

But to build bridges with readers, journalists can't excuse themselves from their local communities. Bridge building requires authentic relationships that can't be cultivated when journalists are prevented from engaging on a human level with the people around them. News leaders appear to be slowly recognizing this. When Americans began hitting the streets to protest in favor of the Black Lives Matter movement following the death of George Floyd in 2020, some news outlets began reexamining their prohibition on journalists participating in public demonstrations. At least one national outlet, *Axios*, decided to allow them to do so.[17]

"What we've got is people who are an aberration in society because they've been restricted in how involved they can be in their community because it will restrict their ability to cover things," Andrews said. "But by being so strict with these conflict-of-interest policies, I think we as a profession appear like we have no interest in things. That's not how the world works." Andrews isn't advocating for unethical journalism in which the journalist fails to disclose potential conflicts. Disclosure is paramount, she said. Simple transparency is what readers and viewers are looking for. "We're, as journalists, always on the outside," Andrews said. "I think we need a reexamining of how journalists can be a fabric of society in the everyday community."

6

From Misunderstanding to Understanding

Water jugs. Leaping friends. A basketball net. A water fountain. A corner store. A dump truck. Shoes.

These are not the types of images you expect to see in a town accustomed to exhibitions of world-class artwork. They are lacking in grandeur and prestige. The subjects of the images are, in fact, noticeably mundane.

Yet these photos are exceptional precisely because they are not exceptional – because they don't take for granted the everyday elements of life and because they force us to look at the world, and each other, from different angles.

Steps away from the Smithsonian Institution's National Portrait Gallery in downtown Washington, DC, these works were displayed at the Pepco Edison Place Gallery in March 2019 for the third annual *Everyday DC* photojournalism exhibition. But unlike the internationally heralded artists featured at the famous museum next door – such as Edgar Degas, George Catlin, and Gilbert Stuart – the artists featured in this gallery were unknown to the world.

They were middle school students from throughout Washington. Seven were chosen to serve as curators for the project, featuring images from 140 student photographers at 14 schools to represent real life in the nation's capital.

126

"Each wall tells a story," curator Shakayla told attendees on opening night.

A person lying face down on flattened cardboard boxes on a cold December day: "Someone looking for a home," wrote Matias of Oyster-Adams Middle School.

A classroom selfie: "This represents everyday DC by showing how nice friends in DC can be," Jonathan of Charles Hart Middle School captioned a photo of himself and his friend Leandre.

A close-up of a girl's hair: "I wanted to capture the texture of my friend's braid," wrote Jefferson Middle School Academy's Kyrah.

The emotions on display in their gallery of framed photos ranged widely, from feelings of helplessness to expressions of joy. These snapshots could have been taken anywhere. And that was the point. The exhibition reflected an intentional effort to demolish stereotypes and build cross-cultural understanding through depictions of mundanity – a sharp contrast to the algorithmically curated stream of images and messages that overwhelm us on social media and collectively skew our perspectives of each other.

The students who participated in *Everyday DC* may be just kids, but they have already observed how digital media have fostered stereotypes of themselves and their hometown. They believe that authentic photography can undercut those misconceptions.

"People in DC are different in many ways," said one of the curators, Jefferson Middle School Academy sixth-grader Shaunea, on opening night, her left arm clasped tightly behind her back and her right arm grasping a microphone. "They have different perspectives and express themselves differently. People show you who they are through movement, through their hairstyles, outfits, the cars they drive, the jobs they have, through the friends they choose and choices they make." Kids in DC, she said, are not what others believe them to be. "Students are dreaming here, changing their minds every day, and showing their emotions. People may still have stereotypes about our District, but in DC you can write your own story, you can choose your own path – and this is ours."

Two hands casting a shadow of a heart: "It shows that there IS love here," wrote Takayla and Lauren of Whittier Education Campus.

A rainbow over a school building: "Rain is not just gloomy," wrote Catie of Eliot-Hine Middle School.

A playground slide: "I was trying to create narrative and atmosphere with this image," wrote Yazmin of Capitol Hill Montessori. "I do not know what the story is yet. When I do, I will tell you."

Shaunea's fellow curator, Jaziah, explained how media reports often perpetuate "misperceptions about DC that we only have government buildings and no one lives here" and perpetuate "stereotypes that we are violent and that people only come to the city for protests."

While contemplating the ways they could use genuine imagery to smash stereotypes, the students also learned the technical aspects of photography and curation, such as framing and symmetry. "You see a lot of diversity through our images," said curator Constance. "DC in the media is all about government, politics, museums, and monuments. That's not what I see in my everyday life."

As dozens of adult attendees surveyed the photos at the student gallery, they placed sticky notes on a black-board with their responses to the following prompt: "According to the media, DC looks like . . ."

"The president"
"Congress"
"Business suits"
"Political chaos!"

"A craven, power hungry, placeless city"
"Nothing but feds and lobbyists"
"An urban jungle"
"Red and blue"
"A mess!"
"Dysfunction"
"Crazy!"

"DC is a city where there's a lot of assumptions made," said Mary Lambert, director of arts for DC Public Schools, which provided support for the exhibition alongside the DC Commission on the Arts and Humanities and the Pulitzer Center on Crisis Reporting. "A lot of people think we're just violent and a big, dirty city, it's just the people who work in politics, and everybody else doesn't matter. So it's a chance for the students to really look at what is our city – the arts and culture that make up who we are."

Everyday DC gave students the opportunity to take control of their narrative. "It's a chance for students across the city to come together, a chance for people to show off the vibrancy of the community and what makes their community special," Lambert said.

A desire to disrupt the narrative is exactly how the movement that inspired the *Everyday DC* exhibition began.

⚹⚹⚹⚹

Like the DC middle school student photographers, journalists Austin Merrill and Peter DiCampo have long been exasperated at how life around them was perceived and portrayed throughout the world. Merrill experienced the disconnect first-hand in Ivory Coast. He did a stint there in the Peace Corps and then moved there in 2002 after grad school to work as a journalist. DiCampo saw it through his own time in the Peace Corps in rural Ghana, where he helped locals fight

Guinea worm disease, a parasitic infection caused by lack of access to clean water.

Despite the challenges of poverty and disease in places like Ivory Coast and Ghana, people's assumptions of life there were wildly off base, the two journalists said. Americans back home would ask them painfully naive questions such as, "Do they have cars? Do they have phones? How are you talking to me right now? How are you on the internet?" DiCampo tried to explain that he actually had "a very normal apartment life" and an ordinary social life in Accra, the capital city of Ghana.

It should come as no surprise that Americans have misperceptions about what life is like across the Atlantic. "We understand what we are shown," DiCampo said. "For Africa, that is really just a lot of war and poverty and famine narrative, and so the expectation is that the entire continent is on fire all the time. And, of course, it's not actually like that."

At one point, Merrill read anthropologist Oscar Lewis's 1959 book, *Five Families: Mexican Case Studies in the Culture of Poverty*, which made an impression on him for its compelling portrayal of the everyday lives of families in Mexico. "I was fascinated with the way in which [Lewis] was able to turn an everyday, normal day – a mundane sort of day – into something that was interesting to read, interesting to learn about, and interesting to immerse yourself in," Merrill said.

Hoping to replicate the same type of storytelling as a professional journalist, he began pursuing feature stories about the daily lives of the people of Ivory Coast. But as he pitched stories to editors back in the United States, his ideas went nowhere. "No one was interested in anything I was interested in trying to write about," he said.

Eventually, Merrill found his way into what he called "the conflict group of reportage in that area," tracking violence in countries such as Sierra Leone and Liberia as a correspondent for the Associated Press. "But the whole time what I was really interested in was trying to find a way to not focus on that stuff and [instead] write about other more normal types of things, even though it's not really news."

After moving to New York City, Merrill got a job at a magazine that allowed him to periodically travel back to Africa. In 2008, he met DiCampo on a trip to Ghana to cover a story about Guinea worm eradication. Merrill was the writer on the story, and DiCampo was the photographer. "We were just trying to do a good job on the story that we did," Merrill said. But afterward, "we stayed in touch and talked about ideas together."

A few years later, they applied for and won a grant from the Pulitzer Center to document Ivory Coast's recovery from years of war, and they traveled to the country in March 2012 to report the story. "It was a story nobody was talking about," Merrill said. "But it was an important piece about a keystone country in west Africa trying to get back on its feet. I was interviewing refugees, and I was interviewing militia soldiers and victims of war crimes and so forth, and [DiCampo] was photographing all these people and places."

In "the process of photojournalism," DiCampo wrote later, "you often feel you 'know' the images needed to tell it. If it's a story with phrases like 'continued ethnic violence,' you feel you need photos of refugees, burned-down homes, survivors with horrific stories to tell, et cetera. These are the images that will make sense to the readers, that they will find palatable."[1]

But at some point during their reporting, they began to realize that their project fit comfortably within the usual catalog of stories and photos that tend to confirm people's stereotypes about life in Africa. "We had this realization that we were piling on," Merrill said. "We had this realization that we got up every morning in a decent hotel – nothing luxurious but perfectly fine – had a perfectly fine breakfast, met our driver, he took us off to wherever it was we had to meet some people to do our story, did our rough-and-tumble reporting and photographing all day long, and then would come back to our fairly decent hotel and have a perfectly nice meal and go to bed."

To be sure, their journalistic angle was on point. "There was nothing inaccurate or misleading about the story we were doing. It was a real thing. But the stuff that no one ever heard about was everything else we were seeing throughout the day," he said.

That's a common experience for American journalists in foreign countries. The story their editors care about is often the one dripping with blood. The everyday moments are frequently ignored. "You know that you need to draw people in, but you don't want to do a disservice to the people that you're reporting on by focusing only on the most extreme narratives," DiCampo said. "By the way that it is constructed, that necessitates driving people apart because you're accentuating what makes people different from each other."

Despite their frustration, DiCampo and Merrill still had a job to do. They were there to report on the fallout from the civil war. But their frustration lingered.

One day, as they ascended an elevator in a government building in Ivory Coast, DiCampo pulled out his iPhone and snapped a photo of what he saw, thinking little of it. It was nothing notable. But as the day went on, he snapped more photos of seemingly mundane moments. "At the end of the day I showed [Merrill] those pictures," DiCampo said. "We thought, there's something to this."

As they continued to report the story they had originally set out to tell, they began experimenting with a new way of documenting life around them. "We started to take our iPhones out of our pockets and tried to find a way to capture those moments, sitting over egg sandwiches in the morning for breakfast, just in a car driving somewhere or street seeing – whatever it was," Merrill said. "In the evenings, we almost found ourselves spending more time swapping those photos back and forth and critiquing them than we did talking about what we were there to do."

A man waiting in an elevator. A woman sitting on a couch with her laptop on a coffee table. An empty office. A man passing by a newsstand. Two men working on a car engine. Someone making a cup of coffee. In many cases, scenes that could be seen practically anywhere.[2] Photos that might appear to say nothing instead said everything. "It was a remarkable difference between the photos that went into the story that we were there to report on and the photos that we made when we freed ourselves from that postwar narrative and just started making pictures of our day as we went through it," DiCampo said. "Very different moments, very different style of photography, and it was interesting that it was all with us in the same place on the same trip. But the cell phone stuff felt a lot more accessible, a lot more familiar."

Upon the trip's conclusion, they began posting their photos on a Tumblr blog titled *Everyday Africa*. The images soon stirred interest among family, friends, and professional contacts. Editors at the *New York Times*, *Business Week*, and elsewhere wanted to publish them. "We started to understand that what we were doing had a power and a novelty," DiCampo said.

Images of everyday life are something we can all identify with. They illuminate what we have in common even as they display our differences. And bridge builders recognize that our differences are what make us human.

After the Ivory Coast project, the two journalists went their separate ways. DiCampo headed to an assignment in Uganda, while Merrill went to cover stories in Nigeria, Zimbabwe, South Africa, and Zambia. But they continued uploading photos to the *Everyday Africa* blog as they traversed the continent.

Following their initial success on Tumblr, they transitioned to Instagram as a more efficient and popular venue for sharing photography. "And it just blew up in a way that we hadn't expected it to at all," Merrill said. The account began adding thousands of followers. And with the extra attention, as Merrill acknowledged, came some natural skepticism about "two American White men" with the audacity to declare "this is everyday Africa." But their hope was to begin dispelling misconceptions, one photo at a time, that White people had been responsible for propagating – and to begin attracting local photographers to take control of their own narrative. And that's exactly what started to happen.

"Some other photographers began to take notice, express some similar frustrations with being forced by the mainstream media outlets to always cover the same kind of poverty and conflict stories, and wanted a way to express themselves about everyday life," Merrill said.

Not long afterward, local photographers throughout Africa were responsible for most of the photos on the account.

⁘

As *Everyday Africa* began picking up steam, the founders traveled to Chicago on behalf of the Pulitzer Center to talk about their project. Speaking to high school students on the city's South Side, Merrill intentionally crafted an uncomfortable inquiry: "Which gangs are you guys in?"

"Whoa, we're not in any gangs," the students protested, according to Merrill's account.

Merrill broke character. "Why do you think I said that?" he asked.

"Because that's what you see in the news," someone responded. "It's not true, we're not in any gangs."

"Then, OK, take a camera, go out in your neighborhood, and come back and tell me what is true," Merrill said. The students went out and did just that.

That's when Merrill and DiCampo began to realize that their project had powerful educational components that could be used to teach students how to communicate and translate the world around them. They soon landed funding from a variety of nonprofits to write curricula for students in the Bronx. The lessons begin with a discussion inspired by *Everyday Africa*.

"You start off by throwing up a map of Africa on the board and saying, 'All right, guys, what's the first thing you think of when I say, "Africa"?'" Merrill said. The responses are predictable. "The kids just start shouting out words, and it's a very common experience for people to say things like 'poverty,' 'hot,' 'elephant,' 'war,' 'slavery,'" Merrill said.

The experience is painfully similar no matter where the program is offered. By middle school, students already have preconceived and often incorrect notions about an entire continent of extraordinarily diverse people – people with different cultures, languages, religions, professions, and life stories.

"Where do these ideas come from? We don't just dream them up. They must come from somewhere," Merrill said. "That's the beginning of a conversation about how do we form our perceptions – where do we get these ideas?"

Social media. News. TV. Movies. Even infomercials for humanitarian efforts.

"We talk about that infamous ... commercial from when I was a kid: 'For fifty cents a day you can save the life of a poor child in Africa.' The way that that burns itself into your brain – it's really unshakeable," Merrill said. Those types of philanthropic efforts may have noble intentions. But the imagery lingers in our minds.

"Even people who feel like this is an attempt to do something good frequently don't realize the ways in which they are being manipulated to think about an entire population of people in a part of the world in a way that's demeaning and disempowering," Merrill said. "You're hardwired to think that children in Africa are poor and starving."

A conversation about those international misconceptions leads into a conversation with students about how people perceive *them*, like the one Merrill carried out in Chicago. "We talk to the kids about a stereotype and what's bad about a stereotype. They usually have a vague idea about what it is," Merrill said. "'Look at these words you just said: poverty. Is there poverty in Africa? Sure. But is it true for everybody? No.' So it's not just stereotypes as inaccurate. It's incomplete."

Those moments of contemplation resonate. "The real light-bulb moment is when they apply that to their own lives," DiCampo said. "They then feel very empowered to take control of their own narrative of their own cities or towns or community."

In one session in the Bronx, students were told to go and photograph the neighborhood around their school. They came back with photos of beautiful architecture, artistic graffiti, and people in a barbershop – no guns, no gangs, no violence. Fourteen-year-old Georgianna Oyol took photos at a flower shop. "I thought to myself, 'Wow, something so pretty in the Bronx,'" she told the *Wall Street Journal* after completing the assignment in 2014. "It would be the last thing someone would expect in the Bronx since the Bronx is stereotyped to be violent and dangerous, when in reality it's like any other place. There are good parts and bad parts."[3]

For the Everyday founders, reaching students is the most effective way to make a long-lasting difference. While kids may have already absorbed stereotypes about the world around them, they are still more likely than intellectually stubborn adults to consider different perspectives.

"If you have a misperception or if you base your assumptions about other people on blunt stereotypes as a ninth grader, some of those ninth graders grow up to be powerful people, whether it's in business, or politics, or other facets of civilization," Merrill said. "And if they continue to harbor those kinds of misperceptions, that can have impacts that ripple out in a wide-arching way. That can have a negative impact on the ways in which countries get along and in which economies function together or don't function together."

Although classroom discussions about current affairs or historical events can be engaging, photography, which is omnipresent due to social media and the smartphone, is the principal medium through which students are learning to see the world. "That is their story of what everyday life is like in their community," Merrill said. "It's giving them agency over their own story instead of giving it to the journalists – the people who frankly are usually a lot like me."

And me.

<hr />

One day, not long after *Everyday Africa* took off, Merrill and DiCampo opened Instagram on their phones. They were taken aback with what they saw. Someone had launched a similar account, *Everyday Asia*, without their permission.

"And it said right there in the tagline: 'inspired by *Everyday Africa*,'" Merrill said. "We had several feelings at once. Part of you is flattered. Part of you is also like, 'Well, hold on a second, I don't know if this is OK for you to be taking my idea.' We realized pretty quickly that it was perfectly OK. Not only was it OK, it was exactly what we wanted. We wanted people to take this idea and run with it."

In the following years, Everyday accounts began popping up throughout the world, such as *Everyday Latin America*, *Everyday Iran*, *Everyday Afghanistan*, *Everyday New Orleans*, and *Everyday Atlanta*. In addition to accounts centered on geographic areas, photographers launched accounts with specific themes, such as *Everyday Climate Change*, *Everyday Incarceration*, and *Everyday Extinction*.

To bring some cohesion to the movement, Merrill and DiCampo brought together some of the account leaders for a week of discussions that culminated in the formation of the nonprofit Everyday Projects, which provides suggested guidelines to people interested in starting their own accounts.

"There's hundreds of them now," Merrill said. "They don't all operate the same way – but all of them in some way are trying to take agency over their own story and trying to find a way to use photography to rise above the stereotypes and misperceptions that the people of those areas are burdened with. And it continues to grow."

✦✦✦✦

What the Everyday accounts have proven is that everyone has a story to tell – and misconceptions to dispel. They just need a platform through which to do so.

From her home in the Baltimore area, Zoshia Minto was becoming increasingly despondent at billowing misconceptions about Islam after terrorists attacked the satirical newspaper *Charlie Hebdo* in Paris in January 2015.[4] The terrorists who carried out the attack had done so in the name of an extremist strain of Islam that was not representative of the religion's followers. But Minto, a practicing Muslim raised by Pakistani parents in America, noticed that the reaction to the attack did not reflect this reality.

"I spent a lot of time online just reading comments, which I probably should not have done, on social media, and I was just struck by the amount of hate and also ignorance," she said. "It was just mindboggling to me, and it hurt." About a month later, three Muslim students were killed in a shooting near the University of North Carolina at Chapel Hill in a possible hate crime.[5] After that incident, Minto, a wedding photographer, wanted to find a way to begin combatting misinformation about Muslims. "My response was to just use photography as a way to create something positive, so that's what I did," she said.

She began seeking out opportunities to present positive images of life as an American Muslim. "I just started photographing," she said. "One of the first pictures I actually made was at a candlelight vigil held in the memory of those three college students. Then I spent many months after that photographing friends and family and attending events and visiting communities and individuals in Washington, DC."

She continued doing this on her own until shortly after the 2016 presidential election, when she was meeting with her mentor Muhammed Muheisen, the Pulitzer Prize-winning photographer who cofounded the *Everyday Refugees* account on Instagram.[6] "I was inspired by what they were doing," Minto said. "It just seemed like a good way to share the images I had been creating. Social media just offers quick access to a lot of people, so I felt like it was a good platform to share these images and hopefully generate some kind of conversation about Muslims and Islam."

That's when she launched the *Everyday American Muslim* account on Instagram. Like *Everyday Africa*, *Everyday Refugees*, and other associated accounts, the photos on the *Everyday American Muslim* feed often display regular daily activities. A woman peering out at the sea in New York. A father braiding his daughter's hair. A woman wearing her abaya and niqab doing yoga in a public park. Minto's father passing campaign signs on his way to vote, shielding himself from the rain with an umbrella.

"There's a number of images on the feed that are actually kind of boring, and that's the point," she said. "There's this [assumption] that we're sitting around in the mosques constantly and fomenting hate and creating this crazy atmosphere where people just want to kill non-Muslims. And that's not what's happening. People are living their daily lives, and that's what's important to them – raising their families, doing something meaningful with their time through their jobs, being active in the community, enjoying time on a beach. Just simple, normal things."

As of August 2020, the account had more than 18,000 followers.[7] One of them was a man from Michigan who reached out to Minto one day after finding the images particularly moving. "He basically just said that he didn't want to fear Muslims, and he appreciated the account and he appreciated seeing these images," Minto said. "It was eye-opening for him. He was opening up to this idea of there being more to Muslims than what's normally shown in TV broadcasts or whatever. We kept up a dialogue, not even necessarily about Muslims or Islam, but just being human."

Sometime after they connected online, they met in person while the man was visiting the East Coast. "We just met up and talked about the project, about pictures, and then just in general, as two normal human beings do," Minto said. "That's the point of the project – to generate this interest from people who might not otherwise know any Muslims. So many people have not met a Muslim before. It was reaffirming in a way."

Minto's goal moving forward is to diversify the *Everyday American Muslim* images. She's conscious of the fact that her group of about nine photographers was based largely on the East Coast at the time I interviewed her. So she's aiming to add photographers in the Midwest, the West, and elsewhere. And she wants to heighten her emphasis on African American Muslims, whom she said are often underrepresented and particularly misunderstood.

"It's sad to say this, but this whole effort is just to humanize Muslims because we've been so dehumanized by people in politics and media," she said. "I just wanted to share daily life, and the hope is that on some level other people would be able to connect with something in common with those images. At the very least, it's a more multidimensional and insightful view of Muslims, instead of the blanket negative view that's cast in the media."

In a discrete way, each photograph posted through the Everyday accounts has a butterfly effect. It winds its way into our collective consciousness, subverting our preconceptions and sparking conversations, both on and off social media, as well as introspection, which collectively serve as accelerants in the bridge building process. When we begin to question our own preexisting views about each other, we are more open to the prospect of forming relationships with and helping people from different walks of life.

"There's a multidirectional reaction," Merrill said. "It becomes this fascinating examination of the depth of the ways in which we misperceive one another."

The overarching goal of the Everyday Projects is to use "social media to actually try to break down some of these silos instead of reinforce them," Merrill said.

But within this context, the evolution of the distribution platform – that is, social media – has become what Jeff Bezos might call a "complexifier."[8] Platforms like Facebook, Instagram, and Twitter give individuals with access to the internet the ability to broadcast messages and images around the world. In the early days of social media, Silicon Valley tech elites told us that their tools would be used to bring the world closer together – to foster interconnectedness and reduce isolation. At first blush, it felt like the essence of democracy.

However, the platforms have evolved to encourage like-minded individuals to group together based on their political, cultural, and social beliefs and heritage, which exacerbates our current divides and paradoxically encourages isolation. This has been worsened by Facebook's introduction of the algorithmic News Feed, which tends to display content that provokes emotional reactions and keeps users coming back for more. Combined with our human tendency to want to be liked, the type of content that tends to surface is sensational, exceptional, or unusual. There's little room for the mundane.

After Instagram began filtering photos based on a similar algorithm, the Facebook-owned social media network risks falling into similar traps as its parent company.[9] For Everyday Projects, the key question is whether it can continue to build digital bridges between people from different areas of the world when it can't control whether Instagram allows its posts to be seen in the feeds of Everyday account followers.

"It's something I'm frustrated with constantly," Merrill said. "I get personally very frustrated with Instagram now because I don't understand why things rise to the top of my queue and I see stuff I don't care about, and stuff I do want to see I don't see."

Conversations with Instagram officials typically yield little insight into the matter, Merrill said. "If you're on a platform like Instagram and an algorithm is deciding what surfaces in your feed, the wrong kind of thing has decided what you should see and what you shouldn't see," he said. "What we're trying to [do is] to encourage curiosity."

And curiosity should be allowed to flourish on social media, even if it doesn't check all the boxes of engagement that typically allow content to make it to the top of the highlight reel. Yet despite natural consternation over the effect of social media on public discourse and people's connections with each other, Merrill continues to believe that social media can be used to bring people together. But it requires a strategic approach to rise above the noise. "Part of the trick is figuring out how to make the mundane absorbing, interesting to look at, noteworthy, whether you're writing a piece of journalism, a piece of fiction, or you're making a photograph or painting," he said.

Bridge builders understand that relationships and verbal conversations can change hearts, but they also understand the power of art to touch the soul and to humanize. "There's a way to celebrate what we have in common. There's a way to use photography to celebrate and to open eyes," Merrill said. "It doesn't mean that's all it should be about – because we're not all the same, and it's crazy to think so. So you're not only celebrating what we have in common, but we're also trying to amplify and appreciate what we don't have in common and embrace those differences."

The amplification factor has a particularly powerful effect through the lens of authentic imagery. The more we see it, the more it opens our eyes. Even the founders of Everyday Projects have experienced the barrier-breaking effects of their own initiative. "I know for myself that there have been moments that I have looked through Everyday accounts and felt like, 'Oh, my god, this is working on me,'" DiCampo said. "Like, I started this thing and I'm still having these moments of, 'I didn't know that happened *there*.'"

As of August 2020, the *Everyday Africa* Instagram account had more than 400,000 followers.[10] Social media made that possible.

"Who knows what it will be in five years?" Merrill said. "Maybe it won't be Instagram anymore. But through the image and through this social media way of sharing images, there's a way to learn something and be engaged and not be as afraid of each other."

Part III

Redrafting the Blueprint of Compromise

There's a reason that American politics increasingly resembles team sports. It's us versus them. Loyalty is paramount. There are winners and losers. Talking heads on TV analyze each maneuver. Fueled by a seemingly unshakable team mentality, politicians cling to members of their respective parties and concoct strategies to demolish their opponents. Back and forth they go. As the game goes on, bitterness often translates into stagnation. The players would rather stand on principle in pursuit of a crushing victory than strike a compromise that allows each side to get something they want for the betterment of society at large.

The parasite of rigidity that has sickened policymaking chambers throughout the country – and especially in Washington – is rooted in a system that rewards party loyalty over pragmatism and practicality. But compromise, the lifeblood of democracy, is what drives political progress in America. Our democracy depends on it. However, with gerrymandered districts dominating the landscape and political fundraising powered by often-secretive donors, elections are typically cornered by candidates who are willing to adopt the least flexible political platform. Limited voter participation in primaries exacerbates the situation. People who actually go to the voting booth on primary day are usually the most ideologically devoted citizens on either side of the aisle. The whole process encourages even mildly centrist candidates to drift leftward or rightward to appeal to the small percentage of the electorate that could actually vote them out. Consequently, there's barely any room in the system for politicians willing to work with the other side. Since elected officials believe there's substantial risk in compromise, they largely refuse to embrace it. Instead, they rest easy in ideologically supercharged bubbles powered by partisan media, rabid followings on social media, and parties that resist structural reform.

147

This is not to say that each side of the political aisle shares an equal portion of the responsibility for systemic polarization. Research from the nonpartisan Brookings Institution suggests that very conservative Republicans are more likely to vote in primary elections than liberal Democrats, thus sending more extreme Republicans to Washington than extreme Democrats.[1] As Brookings scholar Thomas Mann and Norm Ornstein, a scholar at the conservative-leaning American Enterprise Institute, have written, the capital is plagued by "asymmetric polarization," which is due more to severely partisan tactics by Republicans than it is to tactics by Democrats. Recent strong-arm Republican maneuvers have included "using the nation's full faith and credit as a hostage to political demands, shutting down the government, attempting to undermine policies that have been lawfully enacted, blocking nominees not on the basis of their qualifications but to nullify the policies they would pursue, [and] using filibusters as weapons of mass obstruction."[2] What's more, by 2014, consistent liberals were more than twice as likely to endorse compromise than consistent conservatives, according to a Pew Research Center study.[3] Has that changed since then? Possibly – especially in the wake of Donald Trump's presidency and the rise of popular political figures on the left, such as Alexandria Ocasio-Cortez, who have promoted increasingly stiff oppositional stances toward Republican causes. Regardless, while one side may bear more responsibility for our crisis of polarization, neither side can escape responsibility for trying to solve it.

Problematically, though, from a sociological perspective our political system appears almost custom-made to encourage extremism. On a very human level, we are simply not wired to go against the grain. We are wired to group together with people who agree with us because we'd rather remain in the good graces of our friends and colleagues than risk alienation from them. This is a key reason why, for example, Republicans have repeatedly denied the science of climate change, according to Dan Kahan of Yale Law School's Cultural Cognition Project.[4] In many cases, they'd prefer to preserve their elected positions rather than shift their political stances.

The reality is that resurrecting compromise is vital to resolving some of the greatest policy issues of our time. But to do so, we need a wholesale redesigning of the concept itself – both in our legislative chambers and on a personal level. We cannot allow compromise to be extinguished. Rather, it must be elevated and rewarded.

Believe it or not, the seeds of compromise seem to be planted in the ground already, though they are clearly lacking sufficient irrigation. According to a poll conducted in late 2019 by the nonpartisan research group Public Agenda for *USA Today*'s Hidden Common Ground project, 82 percent of Republicans, 67 percent of Democrats, and 76 percent of independents say "there's more common ground between us than the media and politicians say."[5] In other words, people seem to recognize, at least at a conceptual level, that it's possible to bridge some of their political divides.

In an ideal world, perhaps we would overhaul the entire political system from the ground up, fashioning new structures and processes that would foster widespread cooperation. That may be something worth pursuing in the long run. But in the short run, with the balance of power between Republicans and Democrats still roughly even, it's virtually hopeless to wait for a political revolution to take hold. Rather, we need to promote examples of where compromise has led to dynamic change. And we need to encourage reformers embedded within each political party to advocate compromise from within.

This is far easier said than done. But, as you will see in this part, bridge builders are doing it. As facilitators in the pursuit of compromise, their first move is to question the fundamental nature of the process itself. They believe in reimagining what it means to compromise. They believe that people often don't know how to effectively work with one another because of structural hurdles that prevent them from coming together. So they believe in disrupting the status quo by finding new ways of looking at each individual situation. In doing so, they recognize that while compromise may not be the solution to every problem, it is nonetheless crucial for the preservation of our republic.

7

From Denying to Believing

Bob Inglis is used to crossing what his fellow climate-change activists would consider to be enemy lines. He knows the terrain well. He's been a tried-and-true conservative since long before he became a member of Congress in the 1990s and ever since he left in 2010. He still proudly recites his reliably conservative voting record on issues such as abortion.

But Inglis no longer spends his time promoting traditionally right-wing policies. Instead, he regularly tours the country speaking about the climate crisis to conservative groups like the Sea Island Republican Women's Club in Charleston, South Carolina. Inglis arrived at the club in August 2018 as part of a tour organized through republicEn, the nonprofit he founded to inspire his Republican colleagues to accept settled climate-change science and pursue a carbon tax as a bipartisan solution. The former congressman from one of the reddest districts in America – covering Spartanburg and Greenville, South Carolina – was there to speak to members who refer to themselves as "Republican patriots."[1] So he could be forgiven if he was expecting a hostile reception despite his otherwise conservative credentials.

But Inglis has a proven track record of finding common ground with conservatives and using that terrain as a beachhead to deliver his message. He deployed the same strategy at the Sea Island Republican Women's Club. In conversations with the club members before his talk,

Inglis learned that they had recently begun to notice the impact of rising seas on their coastal properties. "We're really concerned about flooding," one member of the club told Inglis before the event began, according to his account. She gestured to the woman next to her. "We're both concerned. In our neighborhood, builders are bringing in hundreds of loads of dirt to lift the foundation level of new houses. Otherwise, the water is going to get into the garages of those new houses."[2]

After hearing their stories, it was Inglis's turn to talk to the group about climate change, which is poised to devastate coastal regions in the coming decades. He tailored his message accordingly. "It doesn't matter whether you're a Republican or a Democrat, red or blue," Inglis told them. "The water is coming up."[3]

He said that friends help each other to see the world the way it is – not the way they believe it to be. A friend wouldn't say, "Don't worry about that water in your yard; I'm sure it's not a problem," Inglis told his fellow Republicans. As he gazed out at the crowd, people were nodding their heads in agreement. Friends, he told the club members, must tell their friends about the importance of fighting climate change.[4]

It was a relatively new friend, in fact, who brought Inglis himself into the fold.

⁂

When Inglis was serving his first three terms in Congress in the 1990s, he didn't believe in climate change. That is, he didn't believe that greenhouse gas emissions – such as carbon dioxide and methane – were forming an atmospheric blanket that traps heat, causing the oceans to rise, triggering extreme weather, ravaging biodiversity, and endangering crops. That version of Bob Inglis was Inglis 1.0, as he later came to say.[5]

After voluntarily relinquishing his seat in 1998 to fulfill a campaign promise, Inglis returned to private life. But he soon got the itch to return to Capitol Hill. In 2004, he waged a successful campaign to recapture his seat. It was in the years following his return to Washington that he began to consider the possibility that climate change was in fact a threat to humanity.

It started with a conversation with his then-18-year-old son, who told him to "clean up your act on the environment."[6] That conversation was a powerful propellant fueling his decision to begin reconsidering his stance on global warming. Soon thereafter, he had the chance to personally witness polar ice melting during a House committee trip to the Arctic, which further nudged him to rethink his position. Still, he wasn't yet ready to join the chorus being sung by climate-change action advocate Al Gore, whom Inglis had actively resisted the previous decade when Gore was vice president.

It wasn't until a voyage Down Under that he finally started to truly believe. During a trip to Australia in 2008 as part of another congressional delegation, Inglis met up with scientist Scott Heron, an expert on the impact of climate change on coral reefs. Heron took Inglis and his tripmates on a snorkeling adventure out of Port Douglas to the Great Barrier Reef.

"We started off with a small group snorkeling, and then some people made the decision to turn back to the boat," Heron recalled in a video interview from his office at James Cook University in Australia, where he is a professor of physics in the College of Science and Engineering. "In the end, it was just Bob and me."

As they dove into the sparkling waters of the Coral Sea, north of Queensland, Heron pointed to the corals below. Back on the surface, he began to explain the urgency of addressing climate change because of the damage it's doing to those oceanic wonders.

"People liken them to the rainforests of the ocean because of their immense biodiversity," Heron told me.

"They also liken them to the canaries in the coal mine – the early-warning markers. And we're seeing those early-warning markers being repeatedly unveiled."

(Bleaching happens when the water becomes too hot, causing corals to lose the microscopic algae they depend on. They then "lose their vibrant colors and turn white" and are more likely to die, thus devastating a critical ocean ecosystem.[7])

Eventually, the conversation turned to their shared Christian faith. Heron explained to Inglis how he lives a life devoted to environmental conservation as a form of worship. For Inglis, it was life-changing to hear someone talk that way.

"I came to faith in college – the 1980s – and at the time, there was a sense of these earth worshipers," Inglis told me. "They were rejecting orthodox beliefs, and therefore we've got to oppose them. That oppositional stance is what defined the operational assumptions of older generations of Christians."

But what Heron helped Inglis see is that environmental conservation doesn't need to take the form of earth worship. As a Christian, Heron believes that the need to address climate change is a spiritual directive of sorts – that corals are "part of creation that we are called to steward," much like you would steward your God-given talents or money.

Inglis began to absorb this mentality as he watched Heron glide above the reef, waiting for him to bubble up to the surface to discuss the exquisite sights below. "I could tell that Scott was not worshiping the corals," Inglis said. "I could tell that he was worshiping the God behind the corals. There was no earth worship going on in Scott."

Soon after returning from his trip to Australia, Inglis took up the climate-change mantle in Congress. He introduced the Raise Wages, Cut Carbon Act of 2009, a revenue-neutral bill that would have slashed Social

Security payroll taxes and implemented a carbon tax. It was a practical attempt at political compromise, designed to appease lawmakers on both sides of the aisle.

It went nowhere. The following year, Inglis lost his Republican primary and thus his seat in Congress. He was jobless – in large part, he says, because the people of his district considered him a heretic for his belief in climate change and his willingness to do something about it.

But Inglis did not let his defeat undermine his commitment to take action. Instead, he resolved to proceed under the premise that convincing conservatives to change their perspectives on climate change is the only way to do something about it. Among Republicans, only 39 percent believe the US government is doing too little to combat climate change, compared with 90 percent of Democrats, according to the Pew Research Center.[8] Such a daunting political divide on climate change requires bridge builders to step into the fray. Without them, the planet is at risk of a meltdown.

Inglis views the pursuit of bipartisan progress on climate change as a pursuit for more than just environmental transformation. "If we're able to successfully address climate change, it may just help us heal the other divisions in our country," he said. "We need a situation in which we pull together to solve a problem."

That attitude reflects a common trait among bridge builders. They filter challenges through a prism of possibility. In this case, the challenge is to show that climate change shouldn't be a partisan issue at all.

The best person to deliver that message to conservatives? Inglis believes it's Republicans themselves because they won't need to walk across hardened political battle lines to get an audience – and because they know best how to speak with each other. That's why he often references one of the country's most beloved conservatives when he speaks to fellow members of the GOP about climate change.

⟪✦✦✦✦⟫

In the final years of the Cold War, President Ronald Reagan took the stage for a speech to an assembly of high school students and teachers in Fallston, Maryland. It was December 4, 1985, and he had recently completed a trip to Geneva, where he had conducted 15 hours of talks with Soviet Union leader Mikhail Gorbachev. During those talks, Reagan discussed his "deep desire for peace" and "a safer and better future" for both Americans and Russians.[9]

It was during those meetings that Reagan brought up aliens. As in, extraterrestrials.

"I couldn't help but say to him, just think how easy his task and mine might be in these meetings that we held if suddenly there was a threat to this world from some other species, from another planet, outside in the universe," Reagan told the high school group, according to a transcript at his presidential library. "We'd forget all the little local differences that we have between our countries, and we would find out once and for all that we really are all human beings here on this earth together. Well, I don't suppose we can wait for some alien race to come down and threaten us, but I think that between us we can bring about that realization."[10]

When Inglis first came upon that clip, he was floored. "It's just sort of like, 'What? President Reagan was talking about aliens threatening us?'" Inglis said.

His disbelief prompted him to explore further. It turns out that Reagan loved the aliens analogy, having used it at least four times. Inglis instructed his team at republicEn to post an audio clip of the speech on the group's website.

It's an odd analogy, but Inglis believes it applies – and that a similar analogy works with climate change.

"Consistent with that theme, this really is something that we're literally all in together," he said. "If this is a place where we could come together and solve it, then it would restore the confidence of Americans that America is the problem solver, is the indispensable nation, and can do good things. It could go beyond climate change, in other words."

To make that vision a reality, however, requires softening the hardened political divide that has formed on climate change. That's why he launched republicEn through the Energy and Enterprise Initiative at George Mason University in Virginia.

In recent years, Inglis has barnstormed some of the most conservative areas of the country, sharing his message with fellow Republicans. His goal is to generate more conservative advocates for a sea change on climate change. By May 2020, he had signed up more than 10,000 people as members of republicEn.

"In raw numbers, it's a small group compared to some other groups," Inglis said. But "we are obviously choosing to try to recruit actual conservatives – because our name is off-putting to everyone else." He laughed at the political reality. Most people who believe in climate change wouldn't be caught dead in a group called republicEn. And that's OK because Inglis doesn't want them in the group. "We're basically saying, 'Love ya if you're a progressive, but we're looking for conservatives.' That sounds contrary to what I was just describing, which is this hope that we're going to bring America together and solve the problem of climate change. But actually there's a method to the madness."

Conservatives, he said, often reject climate change because they can't envision a fix that aligns with their politics. That requires "urging them to go beyond solution aversion, where they just don't think there's a solution that fits with their values. We are showing them there is a solution that fits with their values."

In other words, Inglis is redefining what it means to compromise, much like bridge engineers sometimes need to rethink typical design principles to fit the nuances of a particular construction site. To achieve that goal requires focusing on turning the tide among conservatives, since progressives have already embraced the need to take action. Inglis believes the solution is to explain to conservatives that the free enterprise system can solve climate change by assigning a hefty price to the release of carbon into the atmosphere, which is done through the burning of fossil fuels such as coal, natural gas, and oil.

"We describe ourselves as energy optimists and climate realists. It's an important distinction between that approach and the approach that's been typical in the climate space," which, he said, can place too much emphasis on living with less. "That's OK for some on the left. But it doesn't sell too well on the right."

That type of messaging might not please liberals, but Inglis is taking a purely pragmatic approach. It's the reality of bridge building: sometimes you may need to set aside your political ideals for the sake of action that ultimately brings people together and accomplishes your goals. In this case, for Inglis, it means using highly specific language to draw conservatives into the conversation instead of calling them out for the sake of embarrassing them, which will simply alienate them. "What we talk about is the calling to light up the world with more energy, more mobility, and more freedom," he said.

He believes that conservatives – even Trump supporters – in the reddest parts of America will find appeal in the hope of economic opportunity through an innovation revolution sparked by the need to slash emissions. "What we like to say is that if we play our cards right, we're going to perfect those energy distributions, and we're going to sell that to willing customers around the world, serving them well and creating wealth and jobs in the process here at home. It's a message of abundance," he said.

He understands that critics don't buy it. But he pointed out that skeptics have long underestimated the ability of the free-market economy to accelerate innovation on a global scale. As an example, he recalled a report by the consultancy McKinsey in the early 1980s projecting that the total market for cell phones would eventually top out at 900,000. By the year 1999, it had already reached about 900,000 every three days.[11] Today, of course, they are everywhere.

"So they had missed it by a bit," Inglis joked. But when that projection was made, cell phones, "in fairness to McKinsey, were in bags. They had cords on them, the batteries didn't last, the service was no good, you paid about one dollar a minute for the service. But what happened was the free-enterprise system had competitors who were delivering products to willing customers, and they drove down the prices and they improved the service and they improved the batteries. And the result was that a whole lot of us have a cell phone in our pocket."

That explosion of innovation can happen with energy, too, he said. "We're going to have an energy revolution if we play this right," he said. "And once the free-enterprise system sees the full cost and consumers see the full cost of energy from the burning of fossil fuels, then they will, in the liberty of enlightened self-interest, choose their self-interest by choosing cleaner energy. And the result will be new ways of powering our lives."

It sounds plausible, if not inevitable. But a new tax of any kind is generally a nonstarter on Capitol Hill – certainly while Republicans have enough votes to block any substantive legislation. So how will they ever be convinced to tax carbon? For starters, Inglis believes it's important to emphasize to Republicans that they don't need to compromise their own political values to address the matter. "What we need to do is tell people under the tents in my tribe [that] 'it's completely consistent with your values,'" he said.

To instill that confidence, Inglis emphasizes the concept of accountability, which remains central to the political mentality of many Republicans. "The reason that the incumbent fuels have an advantage against the challenger fuels is that the incumbent fuels aren't accountable for all their cost," he said. "They get away with socializing their soot. They get away with putting their climate damages on the whole of society."

The reality is that coal-fired electricity, for example, appears to be cheap but is actually very expensive when you factor in the damage it's doing to the world, he said.

"A basic belief of conservatism is the concept of accountability and merit and industry and effort and reward following risk," Inglis said. "That's the strength – that's the deliverable – of conservatives in the political process. It's that notion. The deliverable of progressives in the political process is a heavy dose of fairness – let's make sure to make this fair and egalitarian. And the truth is America needs and wants both. . . . It's not like we need to eradicate the other side."

Even if we wanted to, it wouldn't work. Conservatives aren't going away. And neither are liberals. So if we want to do something about climate change, getting through to conservatives might be the only way to achieve progress. And getting through to conservatives probably requires getting through to evangelical Christians, who make up a large chunk of the GOP. Inglis, a fellow Christian who can quote scripture just as easily as he can quote Reagan, talks to them on a regular basis.

"There's only so much depth in political philosophy. But when you go into the realm of faith, it's a much deeper conversation – it's really rich: 'The earth is the Lord's and the fullness thereof,' and, 'The heavens declare the glories of God, and the skies proclaim the work of his hands,'" he said, quoting Psalm 24:1[12] and Psalm 19:1,[13] respectively. "It's really exciting to go there."

But that approach requires challenging what he describes as "this strange view" of "dominion theology" that's "spread among conservative Christians." It derives from the story of Adam and Eve in Genesis, when God tells the first humans that the earth is theirs: "And God said, Let us make man in our image, after our likeness: and let them have dominion over the fish of the sea, and over the fowl of the air, and over the cattle, and over all the earth, and over every creeping thing that creepeth upon the earth."[14]

"Somehow," Inglis said, many Christians believe that passage "means that it's OK to rape and pillage the earth." He rejects that philosophy, saying it does not reflect "the character of God in scripture." Instead, "what you find is a servant God."

Heron, the Australian coral reef expert who has maintained a friendship with Inglis since their transformational snorkeling trip to the Great Barrier Reef, said it shouldn't be a long leap for Christians to make from climate denial or skepticism to acceptance and action. From a practical perspective, Inglis and Heron say it's critical to communicate with Christians – and other members of faith communities – that they don't need to *believe* in climate change in the same way they believe in God or some other higher power.

"It's not actually a belief premise. It's a fact borne out by data. It's data-driven evidence," Heron said. "I would argue the more evidence you can pile about a position of faith, you can consider that to be moving from belief into truism."

From a spiritual perspective, the Christian faith is predicated upon what Jesus said was the second-greatest commandment: "love your neighbor as yourself."[15] "And who's our neighbor?" Heron asked, rhetorically.

"It's the stranger who needs help. That's who our neighbor is. All around the world, there are people that I'm never going to meet who are my global neighbors, and there is a critical importance to live out this aspect of faith in understanding the vulnerability of those people and how that links across to my calling as a Christian."

So when Heron meets the next Bob Inglis 1.0 – that is, the next climate-change denier whose worldview is grounded in a spectrum of faith – he will explain how damage to coral reefs caused by climate change is affecting his neighbors. "That's what the Christian faith should be," Heron said. "We're talking about a half a billion people around the world that have a direct reliance upon coral reefs. They're people. So if the reefs go away, the coastal protection goes away, the protein consumption from fish acquisition goes away – that habitat that it provides. These are examples of how it links to people."

While Inglis acknowledges that it's hard to convince older Christians and, likewise, older Republicans to care about climate change, he said that younger Christians and Republicans are more likely to get it. Research shows he's right. Among millennial Republicans, 52 percent believe the federal government is doing too little to combat climate change, compared with 31 percent of Republican baby-boomers and older members of the GOP.[16] "It's a beautiful thing to see in young believers," Inglis said.

Like many other bridge builders, Inglis believes that America is not trapped in a bottomless pit of polarization. Rather, he believes, the country can be extracted from this free fall. "I think what we're in right now is an aberrant period," he said.

Still, he does get discouraged from time to time about the state of discourse and division in America. In those moments, Inglis – a tried-and-true Republican, mind you – turns to a beloved Democrat for inspiration. He pulls up YouTube and watches John F. Kennedy's speech to Rice University in September 1962, when the president laid out his vision for Americans to go to the moon.

"He admits in the speech that some of this is faith and vision. He also admits that some of the materials needed for the spacecraft hadn't been invented yet. No matter – we're going to the moon before the decade is out," Inglis said.

In the same way, some of the materials needed for bridge building in our polarized world may not exist yet. That doesn't mean we should despair. America's achievement in the space race – putting astronauts on the moon in 1969, when Neil Armstrong took "one giant leap for mankind" – demonstrates what the country is capable of accomplishing when we believe in a common mission, Inglis said.

"You could say, 'Oh, those were better times. America was more united,'" Inglis said. "No way. We had governors in open and willful defiance of desegregation orders. Communism was a real threat. The Cuban Missile Crisis was just about to happen. It's not like he had halcyon days where he could go, 'Oh, sure, we'll bring everyone together.'"

But there was a common enemy: communism. That common enemy caused Americans to do terrible things, including devastating the people of Vietnam, Cambodia, and many in Latin America. However, it also led to the demise of the totalitarian Soviet Union and the destruction of the Berlin Wall, a catalyst of division in Europe. Climate change, Inglis believes, can serve as the next common enemy, not just for Americans but for people throughout the world.

To start making progress, Republicans don't need to agree with Democrats on everything, he said. There's space for conflict to continue to occur. To explain why, he used a metaphor about Ameraucana chickens, which he and his wife raise for eggs at their "farmette" in South Carolina. The color of their eggs looks different to different people. "I see them as sort of green. Others see them as blue. But we've got to have an agreement that an Ameraucana chicken lays eggs," he said. "Whether my eyes perceive green and yours perceive a little bluish – that's OK. But we've got to agree there's an egg there."

Progress, he said, will become evident when Republicans begin turning down the volume of their opposition to climate-change activists. He likens it to disputes among couples. "If you realize you've got the weak end of the argument, volume will make up for it," Inglis said. "And that's what we've got right now – we've got a lot of volume in the political conversation."

Inch by inch, Inglis – that is, Inglis 2.0, as he calls himself now – believes he's helping Republicans turn down the volume. He believes that one day, perhaps sooner than most expect, conservatives and liberals will bridge their divide on this issue.

"What I dream of is a day of moving beyond grudging compromise to creative collaboration," he said. "Grudging compromise is somebody that's trying to grind down an opponent and rub their nose in it. . . . Creative collaboration is where you say, 'So we've got some good ideas, and you've got some good ideas – let's see if we can get them together.' And I think that is what climate change can be."

8

From Rigidity to Flexibility

For Thomas Stallworth III's entire life, the Motor City had been shrinking.

Stallworth was born in Detroit in 1956, shortly after the city's population peaked at 1.85 million residents. As a student at Mumford High School on Detroit's northwest side, he got interested in social activism when administrators were implementing budget cuts as a result of the city's economic decline, which would continue unabated for several decades to come.

"My first real involvement in politics was, to be honest, leading a school sleep-in because the schools were cutting teachers," he said. "From there, I grew into, and I guess am a product of, the Black Power movement, which was a real racial and cultural awakening for African Americans. That just piqued my interest in the need for change."

Political activism ran in his family. His mother, Alma, served a quarter century as a Democratic member of the state legislature at a time when Michigan had no term limits. As one of the first Black female lawmakers in the state capital of Lansing, she struck political compromises with her Republican colleagues on issues such as utility reform to protect poor Michiganders from power shutoffs.

"She was a trailblazer," Stallworth said. "She was able to get stuff done by pulling people together. She's a humble person – she comes from humble beginnings.

But she was and is a bridge builder. So everything that I am politically is a result of her influence and having had the blessing and opportunity to learn from her."

After graduating from college, he got into a management training program through an affirmative action initiative at grocery chain A&P. There, his older boss Eugene, a White man from Lexington, Kentucky, initially refused to acknowledge him.

"There was a lot of resentment," Stallworth said. "I didn't come up through the ranks. I came out of college. This guy did not speak to me, didn't give me any direction for like 90 straight days. I was going to work every day, and the guy wouldn't talk to me. Believe it or not, I was just really heartbroken. I was hurt. I was angry."

Stallworth's wife eventually encouraged him to extend an olive branch to Eugene. "God only knows what made her think of this, but she said, 'Why don't you invite him over for dinner?' I was like, 'What? I'll try it, honey, but I don't think he's going to [accept],'" Stallworth said. "I approached him. I was like, 'My wife would like to invite you over for dinner.' And he accepted."

Eugene came over to their home for a pot-roast meal. "Once he got there and he saw us as a family sitting there at the dinner table, I don't know what he thought," Stallworth said. "But we had dinner, and he got very, very comfortable. We began to talk about his life and his family, talk about mine. And we found common ground."

From then on, their relationship in the workplace was smooth sailing. "I only share that story because it shaped how I enter the room when I'm in a minority position," Stallworth said. "It helped me understand people." It helped him understand the power of relationships to overcome even the widest of divides.

In 2010, Stallworth was elected to the Michigan House of Representatives from the district that included his high school, the University of Detroit, and the Detroit Medical Center's Sinai-Grace Hospital. Less than a year after his reelection to a second term, the city of Detroit filed the largest Chapter 9 municipal bankruptcy petition in US history on July 18, 2013.[1]

Detroit's population had plummeted to below 700,000. The city – which had helped preserve freedom for the world as the Arsenal of Democracy during World War II, put America on wheels, helped create the middle class, and inspired listeners with its groundbreaking music – had fallen deeply into disrepair. Among the many reasons: the US auto industry's globalization and subsequent collapse, state disinvestment, racism in many forms, White flight, poor schools, rampant crime, predatory lenders, excessive borrowing, and political corruption.[2]

To be sure, the city's downtown and Midtown neighborhoods had been enjoying a renaissance of sorts, but the budding comeback had not spread far beyond those limited boundaries in a city with enough land to fit San Francisco, Boston, and Manhattan combined. The fiscal calamity had plunged most of Detroit's neighborhoods into poverty and chaos, spawning a humanitarian crisis in the richest country in the world. About 40 percent of the city's streetlights were out. Police were taking an average of more than half an hour to get to the scene of major crimes. The bus transit system was shattered. Jobs were scarce. Public schools were abysmal. Tens of thousands of abandoned homes and commercial properties littered the landscape.[3]

The pain had intensified when Michigan Governor Rick Snyder appointed bankruptcy attorney Kevyn Orr in March 2013 as emergency manager to take over the Detroit city government with marching orders to fix the municipality's brutal balance sheet. After a few months on the job, Orr sent Detroit into bankruptcy, describing the process as the best way for the city to get back on its feet despite the painful cuts that would likely be necessary for its creditors.

"I really didn't know what to think or feel," Stallworth told me when we met on an unusually snow-free winter evening in Detroit several years later. "I mean, I'm not an attorney. I haven't been through a bankruptcy. I knew very little about municipal bankruptcies."

He interrupted his comments to take off his Detroit Tigers baseball cap, revealing his closely cropped salt-and-pepper hair. "Quite frankly, the financial troubles of Detroit have been going on for decades, so it wasn't like that part of it was a surprise," he said. "So with the initial announcement, I can't honestly say I was shocked."

As part of the bankruptcy, Orr threatened to slash the retirement benefits of the city's 32,000 pensioners. Pension cuts of about 32 percent suddenly became a possibility under his proposal.[4] There simply wasn't enough money to pay them in full, the emergency manager contended. Detroit could no longer afford to make promises it could not keep.

"I was scared that people who had worked all their lives for pensions would be harmed in such a drastic way that they could very easily have been pushed over the edge into poverty or have to return to work," Stallworth said, adding that the fear was particularly palpable for him because his parents both had government pensions.

He resolved to do something about the bankruptcy. But how? Detroit was swamped with $18 billion in debt – far more than the city could ever repay to its about 170,000 creditors, a startling figure that prompted US bankruptcy Judge Steven Rhodes to rule it was "impracticable" for the city to negotiate in good faith without bankruptcy protection.[5]

In other words, Detroit didn't even have the time or wherewithal to talk with its creditors about how broke it was. And yet arguing is all that many people – bondholders, bankers, lawyers, retirees, residents, Republicans, Democrats – wanted to do when the case erupted. The fight over what to do about the bankruptcy was drowned out by people fighting over what led to the bankruptcy. How could this happen? Who was to blame? All quite natural questions. And certainly relevant.

But the debate deepened the usual political divisions in Michigan, where tension among Democrats and Republicans had calcified – White versus Black, suburban versus urban, conservative versus liberal. In a way, Michigan's divides mirrored the country's divides.

"My constituents were ... disenfranchised. They were struggling. They didn't feel like they had the opportunities that others had. And they felt like it was a constructed lack of opportunity – it wasn't by accident," Stallworth said. In other words, the White, conservative business and political establishment had exploited Detroit for decades, contributing directly to the crisis that spawned the bankruptcy filing. "So they were largely angry – angry at Lansing, angry at the suburbs, angry because they felt like Detroit was being robbed of opportunities that it was deserving of," Stallworth said. "And some of that anger probably is justified."

Many of Stallworth's Democratic colleagues in the state legislature shared those perspectives: "If the state had given us our revenue sharing, if they hadn't taken over the schools, if business hadn't left – it's all racism," Stallworth said, summarizing the discontentment. "There was a lot of finger pointing."

Republicans – especially those in Detroit's wealthy White suburbs, which had clashed with the city for decades – focused their criticism on the bankrupt government's corruption, its borrowing binge, and its failure to steward state resources effectively. "Anytime I talk about Detroit, it will not be positive. Therefore, I'm called a Detroit basher. The truth hurts, you know? Tough shit," said longtime Detroit critic and Republican politician L. Brooks Patterson, who was then the top elected official in Oakland County, a mostly affluent collection of cities north of Detroit that were the destination of many White people who fled Detroit over the years. The late Patterson's remarks, published in a *New Yorker* profile[6] during the bankruptcy while he was still in power, were viewed locally as reflective of the bitter and longstanding divide between Detroit and its suburbs.

Much of the long-running feud stems from the region's status as one of the most segregated areas of the country.[7] In the decades leading up to the bankruptcy, White flight and discriminatory real estate practices devastated the city while enriching the suburbs, fueling the region's racial, political, and social divides. For example, about half an hour to the city's west is the city of Livonia, which is often referred to as one of the largest almost entirely White cities in America. Of Livonia's 94,000 residents, about nine in ten are White.[8] In Detroit, about eight in ten residents are Black.[9] One recent analysis of social, racial, economic, and household diversity covering more than 300 American cities ranked Livonia as second to last and Detroit as last.[10]

Which is why it was especially stunning when a White legislator from Livonia and a Black legislator from Detroit became the leading legislative proponents of a compromise to help resolve the bankruptcy and get the Motor City back on its feet.

⁕⁕⁕⁕

John Walsh's interest in Republican politics dates back to his high school days in Livonia, when he did an internship in 1979 with Republican lawmaker Jack Kirksey, who represented the area in the Michigan House and later became mayor of his hometown. It was during that period that Walsh learned the importance of relationships across political and social boundaries. "There was an aura of working together, and they served longer and knew each other," Walsh said of past legislators. "It was harder to vilify one another when you were having dinner or drinks or knowing each other's kids."

In college, Walsh would often discuss politics with his father on long-distance calls. "He'd say, 'Did you hear about such and such?' He goes, 'If I had money, I'd send you to Washington right now, and you'd fix it,'" Walsh recalled. His interest in becoming a state legislator "really started from these conversations that we had as a family" and from his internship. "I just had an exposure to Lansing and felt someday I would go there."

Like many people in the region, Walsh's family has roots in Detroit. His mom grew up in Detroit's Rosedale neighborhood. She was living there when she met his dad, who was briefly stationed in Detroit for the US military before he shipped out to the Pacific during World War II. "So I just had an affinity for the city," Walsh said.

Walsh's career as a lawyer initially took him to a job at a firm in Detroit. Later, he became an executive at Livonia's Schoolcraft College, where he was working when Michigan lawmakers were seeking a solution to the state's fiscal crisis in the midst of the auto industry's collapse. "It was 2008, and Republicans and Democrats came together and raised our income tax. The goal was to eliminate our deficit, which I thought to myself, 'This is a good idea,'" he said. "They did it. And then they increased spending in the next budget. To this day, it still makes the hair on my neck stand. So I decided there was an open seat and it was time to go to Lansing because I knew things were only going to get worse, and I really wanted to try and do something."

In 2008, Walsh was elected to the House to represent the district made up solely of Livonia, which is on the western edge of Wayne County. Two years later, he was joined in the House by Stallworth, representing Detroit, which is on the eastern edge of Wayne County. They didn't know each other well at first. But on the floor of the House, they didn't stay on their own sides of the political aisle.

"I just remember you would come over and chat," Walsh said, glancing over at Stallworth on the second-floor lounge of the Detroit hotel where I got them together for a reunion. "You didn't stay on your side and say, 'We got this.'" Walsh's light-gray suit jacket and customary blue collared shirt reflected his typically thoughtful and subdued cadence in conversation.

"John was always quiet and reserved. I could tell he's about his business," Stallworth said. There was a pause. "Which is kind of like what I was," he continued, delivering the punch line with a shoulder-shaking laugh. Walsh grinned widely. "Tom was an easy guy just to get to know."

That doesn't mean they had much in common. After all, the political and racial divide between Livonia and Detroit is vast. And their respective upbringings took them on a long arc to vastly different political stances, even though they were both born in the Motor City.

But what they had in common was a basic humanity that they recognized in each other. In their conversations together, they spent just as much time trying to understand each other as they did trying to be understood – a hallmark of effective bridge building.

"For me, it's listening. It's a lost art," Walsh said. "I try to spend more time listening than I do talking, if I can, and really understand where they're coming from. You'll get to common ground if you're just patient and never, ever lose focus of loving another human being. Even if you disagree. I find that calms people."

Stallworth said he approaches problem-solving by withholding judgment about his opponent. "It's so hard to reach agreement when people feel like they're being judged. So you have to separate the opinion and the issue from the person," he said. "They may disagree with you – that doesn't make them a bad person. They may be a complete idiot – it doesn't make them a bad person."

As they got to know each other better, Walsh and Stallworth started to form a closer relationship against the backdrop of their shared ties to Wayne County.

Their relationship would soon change the course of Detroit's history.

✦✦✦✦✦

When the Detroit bankruptcy began, there was no reason to believe that the state capital's culture of finding plenty of blame and very few solutions would change. If anything, it seemed more likely that political paralysis would prevail in Lansing as Republicans blamed Democrats for pervasive mismanagement and Democrats blamed Republicans for preserving the suburbs over the city.

"It's your fault. No, it's your fault" – that was the essence of the conversation, Walsh said. And there was "some accuracy and inaccuracy in all of it."

Among Stallworth's fellow Democrats in the state House, the focus was on how to prevent the city's retirees from harm. "Nobody runs for office because they want people to suffer," he said. "We're all sitting there going, 'Well, what are we going to do?' A lot of folks really just didn't even understand all the moving parts of it. It was a very, very complex situation."

"Extraordinarily so," Walsh added.

That's one reason why the bankruptcy was ultimately necessary, they both agreed. How else to provide Detroit with the legal ability to slash its debts, which required payments representing more than 40 percent of the city's annual budget heading into the bankruptcy.[11] That's money that wasn't being spent on basic services to benefit residents, like garbage pickup, park cleanup, and public safety.

When the case started, Walsh felt like "some relief" was in order to unburden the city from its substantial debt load. But that doesn't mean he was eager to take up the mantle of pursuing a resolution. "We were rubbing our hands, saying, 'What the hell are we going to do?' Because I don't care if you lived in Redford or Marquette or if you were a Republican or a Democrat, it didn't matter – no one wanted to" tackle legislation to address the crisis, he said, referring to Michigan towns that are about 450 miles apart.

In other words, lawmakers didn't want to put their careers at risk to pursue a legislative fix to the bankruptcy. That's standard procedure in politics, where the crown of party loyalty typically is prized while compromise is shunned. But bridge builders don't let fear guide their actions. They view compromise as a concept that can be strategically molded to better appeal to divided people.

Walsh already had a reputation in Lansing for teaming with Detroit Democrats on House bills related to the city. They were "small issues," to be sure, but "we got into a habit of cosponsoring the bills. A Detroiter and I would cosponsor one, so that we'd have a Republican and a Democrat," Walsh said. As a result, Governor Snyder and Republican Speaker Jase Bolger asked Walsh to take the lead in pursuing a legislative contribution to help end the bankruptcy.

After Walsh agreed to do so, he quickly formed a bipartisan partnership with Stallworth, hoping to translate their working relationship into a tangible resolution for Detroit. Meanwhile, separate from their legislative efforts, they got assistance from the bankruptcy's lead

mediator, US District Court Judge Gerald Rosen, who
secured unprecedented pledges worth several hundred
million dollars from major philanthropic foundations
and individual donors to help reduce pension cuts and
preserve a city-owned art museum from potential liq-
uidation.[12] But that deal, which came to be known as
the "grand bargain" in Detroit, was contingent upon
Walsh and Stallworth winning the passage of a pack-
age of bipartisan bills in the state legislature – at a time
when knee-jerk partisanship was a more natural political response. The most critical component of the state
legislation was a proposed contribution valued at $350
million over 20 years. In exchange, the bulk of Detroit's
pensioners would face cuts of about 4.5 percent, significantly reduced from Orr's initial proposal of 32
percent.[13]

For Republicans, it required risking criticism of providing Detroit with a bailout. And for Democrats, it
required subjecting themselves to criticism that they
caved in instead of fighting for the rights of pensioners
who didn't deserve to sacrifice at all.

Walsh and Stallworth set aside political idealism in
favor of pragmatism to persuade their colleagues on
both sides of the aisle. For Walsh, it meant explaining
to Republican legislators that the ripple effects of the
bankruptcy would harm pensioners in Detroit but also
city retirees living elsewhere in the state.

"I love data. We used the Treasury Department
heavily. We broke down lists like crazy," said Walsh,
his eyes lighting up at the wonky memory. "I could tell
you how many Detroit pensioners were in almost every
district."

"We did have that number," Stallworth recalled.

"We'd go together or separately [and] meet with
members. We'd meet with their citizens if they asked us
to," Walsh said.

For Stallworth, the challenge was to convince his

fellow Democrats to set aside their anger and admit the reality: Detroit was broke, and no amount of blame or arguing about the situation would change that. "We didn't have the assets," he said.

Armed with the sobering numbers and an emotional appeal to compromise to help Detroit get back on its feet, Stallworth met with various stakeholders at an office in downtown Detroit. "I marched them in – labor, the bondholders, constituents, the folks representing the pensioners, pension board members. And I did it with as many of our Detroit caucus members as would participate," he said. "We sat there three straight days just talking to folks."

Those conversations, on each side of the aisle, began to nudge legislators toward compromise. Perhaps most importantly, Walsh and Stallworth began taking hardened lawmakers to Detroit for tours of how the city had suffered over time from a lack of investment in basic services. That forced them to come face-to-face with the human impact of the city's overwhelming debt, which would be slashed by several billion dollars if the grand bargain was approved as part of a broader bankruptcy restructuring plan.

Bridge builders don't shy away from reality. They don't paper over the past. They educate people about it.

"We would keep getting vans and bringing members down – Republicans and Democrats – to visit the city. So it wasn't just numbers anymore," Walsh said.

The visceral nature of the city's rampant blight and poverty was impossible to ignore. "That made a big difference," Stallworth said.

Walsh made a practical appeal to state Republicans, arguing that they should make the contribution to Detroit to avoid the possibility of accruing a massive legal liability if the pension cuts were later overturned in court. And Stallworth helped his colleagues see that they weren't compromising their identity as Democrats by embracing a political compromise with the other side of the aisle.

"Somehow – I can't tell you the day – the tide changed," Walsh said. "People started just believing."

"Often times people operate out of fear, out of ignorance," Stallworth added. "You can reach them if you find common ground."

Bridge builders don't need to relinquish their political ideals. If anything, they can and should proudly display their values. But to reach common ground, they spurn political, social, and cultural tribalism, which fuels the divide that makes political compromise so difficult to achieve in this country. They recognize that they can't stay entrenched in their own camps if they want to bring about change.

"What I do try to do," Stallworth said, "is move amongst tribes."

~~~~~

In June 2014, the Michigan legislature passed the necessary bills to authorize the grand bargain, including the state's financial contribution, by a wide margin. Cheers erupted after the legislation crossed the finish line in a sweeping bipartisan compromise.[14]

Not everyone was on board, of course. A handful of Republicans and a handful of Democrats refused to sign on. "There were a few stragglers," Stallworth said. But the bitter disagreements over Detroit's past had given way, at least among the broad coalition of grand bargain supporters, to a hope "for better things," as the city's motto goes.

The legislative vote helped end the bankruptcy, giving Detroit the ability to begin investing the extra cash flow it gained from debt cuts to improve basic city services, such as public safety equipment, blight removal, street lighting upgrades, parks improvements, and new buses. The bankruptcy also restored investors' faith in the city government, fueling new projects throughout Detroit's primary business districts.[15] While a truly inclusive recovery is likely to take many years – after all, it took the city several decades to fall into despair – the bankruptcy placed Detroit on a path toward reinvention.

To be sure, metro Detroit's historical divide along racial lines and political boundaries has "very deep roots" that won't go away any time soon, if ever, Stallworth acknowledged. "But I tend to believe that we all want the same thing – we want a safe, vibrant community, a good place to raise our kids, a good education system, a job where we can pay our bills."

And yet anger continues to linger in some quarters about the grand bargain, despite signs since the bankruptcy that Detroit is slowly getting back on its feet. Bondholders remain upset that they had to endure reductions, while many pensioners remain angry that they, too, had to accept cuts, Stallworth and Walsh noted. "You're not a hero when you make the cut smaller," Stallworth said. "There were a lot of people that were very angry with me." The grand bargain was not a perfect solution, he acknowledged. But imperfection constitutes the nucleus of compromise. And compromise is the fuel that keeps American democracy running – even if it may not win elections.

Bridge builders recognize that compromise can occur without undermining one's values. But they also recognize that it sometimes comes with short-term consequences, even if people eventually come to embrace the decision in the long run.

As the grand bargain legislation was coming together, Stallworth was concurrently immersed in a competitive primary campaign for a state Senate seat. Several of his opponents relentlessly bashed his support of the grand bargain, saying that he had failed to serve the best interests of his constituents.

About two months after the legislation was approved, Stallworth lost the race. His political career was over. While he could not pinpoint the precise reasons for his loss in the competitive race, he wondered if his decision to compromise to help end the Detroit bankruptcy played a role.

"When I first was elected, every community meeting I went to, I would do a little poll," he said. "I would say, 'Well, listen, up in Lansing there's going to be times when legislation is moving that you're not going to like and maybe believe is pretty bad and harmful. And in those instances, would you prefer I work to drive a compromise and minimize harm, or would you prefer me to fight to the end, go down in flames?'"

The response was usually the same.

"Nine out of ten people said, 'Go down in flames. Stand on principle,'" Stallworth recalled. "Despite minimizing harm, you're viewed sometimes as a sellout because you didn't stand on principle."

That's not a view specific to Detroit, or to Stallworth's district, or to Democrats, or to Republicans. It's characteristic of our fiercely polarized political culture. Adhering to a rigid ideological framework is often more efficient than brokering compromises for the betterment of the electorate as a whole. That's what makes the work of bridge building so strenuous. It goes against the grain.

The spans of policy progress often can't be built without temporarily angering people with long stretches of orange barrels, which are often enough to make people lose sight of the road improvements they'll enjoy when it's all over. But bridge builders nonetheless embrace congestion.

"Honestly, I just feel like if you're really, sincerely committed to serving people – to public service – you make the right choices for the right reasons," Stallworth said. "But I don't think people understand the work and sacrifice that's required to get to a compromise. It doesn't just *happen*."

"It takes work," Walsh interjected.

Stallworth repeated him without missing a beat. "It takes work."

9

From Discord to Collaboration

If you haven't noticed, we live in a hot-take culture. On social media, on cable TV, in partisan media, in the mainstream press, in politics, we are saturated with opinions. We are constantly told what to believe, whom to believe, and how to believe. And we are often eager to fire off our own missives, betraying nuance for the sake of embarrassing others.

Amid the cacophony of discord, it's becoming increasingly difficult to find people who willingly set aside their personal feelings for the sake of helping others reach a consensus. It takes skill and experience to remove your emotions from the equation and attempt to help resolve a conflict objectively. It's uncomfortable and, therefore, quite unusual.

Yet that's precisely what professional mediators are trained to do. Unlike judges or arbitrators, mediators don't issue rulings. Instead, they analyze issues logically, help all sides understand the strengths and weaknesses of their positions, and present solutions that everyone can embrace.

Through their experiences mediating legal disputes outside of court, settling conflicts inside the workplace, and resolving divides within families, Steven Dinkin and Lisa Maxwell, leaders of the San Diego-based National Conflict Resolution Center (NCRC), have become expert bridge builders in the most practical sense of the term. They facilitate amicable resolutions through negotiations in high-stakes settings such as the US military and in off-the-radar situations such as marriages and small businesses. In doing so, the NCRC leaders have developed invaluable insights on how to bring fighting parties together. The principles of mediation, they said, can be applied in everyday life, even when an actual mediator would never be used.

Effective mediators aren't simply trying to figure out "how to split the baby" by divvying up resources, Maxwell said, referring to the biblical story of King Solomon's wise proposal to resolve a dispute between two women who both claimed to be the true mother of a child. The real one revealed herself by offering to give up the baby to the imposter, rather than see the baby halved.[1]

With apologies to Solomon, simply splitting the baby is insufficient. The critical question for people in the midst of conflict is, "How can we move forward together in an ongoing relationship?" said Maxwell, who serves as director of NCRC's Training Institute.

That mentality requires initiating dialogue about difficult subjects without dwelling on complaints about the situation. "You can transform a conversation by, instead of looking at whose fault it is, you look at what each person's needs involve," Maxwell said. "Were they hoping for respect? Were they hoping for fairness or input – basic things that are important to us as human beings? It helps us see conflict differently – much more from an empathetic and compassionate perspective."

The concept of mediating a conflict without first determining which side deserves the most blame is decidedly antithetical to our hot-take culture, which teaches us to point fingers and excoriate others for their failures. But the countercultural principles of mediation can serve as an effective antidote to the paralysis often caused by conflict.

"It's bringing individuals together with a different set of viewpoints and different perspectives and having them work through a challenging issue to come to a solution. The essence of that is dialogue," said Dinkin, NCRC's president. "Because we are so polarized, there's not as many opportunities to engage in that type of dialogue because people are staying in their own silos. And when there are contentious issues, rather than engaging in dialogue, they're turning away from that."

We tend to reject the antidote by rushing into our isolated digital corners, gushing intolerance, and self-segregating ourselves in real life to avoid interacting with people who aren't like us. Consequently, disruptive conflict is inevitable whenever we come into contact with people from the other side. "The concept of actually bringing people together with different points of view – that is not where society is resting right now," Dinkin said.

And yet that is exactly what NCRC is doing.

In the 1970s and 1980s, a nationwide push following the Civil Rights Movement led to the creation of neighborhood justice centers and community mediation centers throughout the country to help marginalized people gain access to legal tools they otherwise couldn't afford. Centers formed in places such as Atlanta, Kansas City, Los Angeles, San Francisco, Manhattan, Honolulu, Dallas, and San Diego. In many cases, a portion of court-filing fees was set aside to enable the centers to offer free mediation services.[2]

By 2011, there were some 400 such centers throughout the country. With an average budget of less than $200,000, however, the typical center's community impact was relatively limited. And with many financially strapped governments having slashed funding, job cuts and reduced services had left many community mediation centers with insufficient resources to achieve their missions.[3]

Like other similar organizations, the San Diego Mediation Center was in a financially precarious position in 2003, when Dinkin joined. Formed 20 years earlier, the center had been helping resolve disputes between a variety of parties, including landlords and tenants, parents and teenagers, and consumers and merchants. But when Dinkin came on board, as much as 65 percent of the organization's funding came from the court system, making it extremely reliant on unstable governmental support to continue operating.

Recognizing the need to diversify the organization's revenue, Dinkin began extending the group's services into other areas, such as personal injury cases, medical malpractice, business partnership dissolutions, divorces, and probate matters. As its expansion took hold, the organization changed its name in 2005 to the National Conflict Resolution Center.

Meanwhile, NCRC leaders began realizing that mediation was enticing to people throughout the country, but there were not enough mediators to go around. So NCRC formed its Training Institute, which helps individuals such as attorneys, retired judges, and community members learn how to conduct mediation sessions. In addition, the group began creating courses designed to translate the principles of successful dispute resolution into training sessions for employers throughout the world to help people mitigate conflicts in the workplace.

The workshops promote early intervention, empowering workers, families, and community members to stave off clashes before they become serious. "The idea is that if we really want to have an impact on society and change the culture to create a more civil society, we wanted to put into the hands of thousands and thousands of people the tool sets of mediation – the powerful strategy of conflict resolution and communication – so they can proactively resolve those disputes before they escalate to the point where they even need to go through formal mediation," Dinkin said.

The nonprofit's expansion into various forms of alternative dispute resolution, the addition of mediator training, and the creation of training programs have placed NCRC on a sustainable financial path. Corporate contracts, federal government deals, fee-for-service mediation, and philanthropic donations have flooded in, expanding the group's annual budget to nearly $4.6 million, according to the most recently available tax documents.[4] In 2019, only about 10 percent of the group's funding came from courts, Dinkin said.

"We are working with homeless veterans and then also with very sophisticated workers in large Fortune 500 companies," Dinkin said. "It's the breadth of our work and expansiveness of our work that's so unique."

⁜

One key reason why the nonprofit has gained momentum is because of the purely practical benefits of mediation. For starters, it can be significantly cheaper and faster than litigation. For example, the average divorce mediated by NCRC costs about $4,300 to $8,000 for each party, compared with attorney fees per party of about $42,000 for a similar case involving two court hearings and mid-range legal costs.[5] And to San Diego residents in certain cases, the mediation process is free.

"The court system is increasingly clogged, so if you get caught up in the court system, you could be locked in there for an extended period of time, where mediation is much more expedient," Dinkin said.

One common alternative is arbitration. But heightened awareness of the perils of arbitration is causing many watchdogs to question the process, particularly when employers or merchants use contractual language to force workers or consumers into arbitration against their wishes. Forcible arbitration, when paired with confidentiality clauses, can also enable people who have committed certain offenses, such as sexual misconduct, to hide their wrongdoing and escape consequences in the future.[6] In contrast, negotiating parties can walk away in the middle of mediation without being forced to stay silent.

More than 56 percent of American nonunionized private-sector workers are subject to mandatory employment arbitration in the event of a dispute with their employer. That's up from 2 percent in 1992, according to the Economic Policy Institute.[7] The balance of justice is tipped against workers in arbitration proceedings, as well. In fact, employees are about 2.6 times more likely to win their cases in state courts than in arbitration and 1.7 times more likely to win in federal courts.[8]

Unlike the typical arbitration proceeding, mediation is voluntary. That means you're not obligated to reach a resolution, unlike arbitration, which requires participants to adhere to the final decision once they've entered into the process.

Another benefit of the mediation process is that it's typically less contentious than court proceedings. Rather than a zero-sum outcome, each side is encouraged to see the other's perspective and reach a mutually satisfactory result. "It tends to preserve relationships – especially in situations where there's going to be an ongoing relationship, like in a situation where there's a divorce and there's custody issues," Dinkin said. "If you go through divorce mediation, you're still going to get divorced, but it won't be as acrimonious, so you'll be able to preserve a relationship enough where you can deal with the children."

In 2019, NCRC, which does not practice arbitration, mediated more than 1,400 disputes – of which 80 percent ended with settlements – and trained more than 10,000 people worldwide.[9]

Armed with the principles of professional mediation, NCRC has sought to extend its model into the public square. The increasingly belligerent nature of public discourse led the group to launch a campaign to promote civil interaction in government and schools. On college campuses, the organization is training thousands of students on "how to be more inclusive and how to communicate across differences," Dinkin said.

The move came amid an eruption in toxic interactions on college campuses involving free-speech rights and clashes between people from opposite ends of the political and cultural spectrums. College students are generally taught how to effectively advocate for themselves, which is a good thing, but they are not typically taught how to dwell in community with people of political difference, Maxwell said. "It's one thing to stand up for one's rights and one's identity, but sometimes they leave those conversations feeling more upset," she said.

At San Diego State University, more than 950 students had recently completed NCRC's civil discourse training when I interviewed the group's leaders. Afterward, course evaluations showed that nearly all the participants enjoyed increased "confidence in addressing conflict in their communities," improved "ability to address the conflict style of others to achieve their own goals," and heightened "willingness to speak up when they witness discrimination." Before the program, the university administration had been asked to resolve "dozens of disputes" on campus per academic year. In the first full year following the NCRC training, that figure dropped to two.[10]

One recent evolution of NCRC's emphasis on helping college campuses promote civil discourse is a program to train what it calls "dialogue ambassadors." At the University of California San Diego (UCSD), where the initiative was launched, NCRC trained student leaders on how to conduct dialogue through the circle discussion process. This technique of promoting productive conversation – also used by the group Coming to the Table featured in Chapter 1 – is based on the principles of restorative justice.

"We've trained the students as facilitators, and now they're leading circle dialogues on the college campus around very challenging issues," Dinkin said. "They bring students together with opposing points of view."

It's especially critical to educate students on how to interact with others who aren't like them because colleges can be a breeding ground for ideological and cultural segregation, as students often congregate in clubs that lack diversity, Dinkin said. "Those students would just stay within their clubs, and they wouldn't interact with other students," he said. "What we're trying to do is to have them go through training where they learn fundamental communication skills. They learn about their own identity. They learn about the identity of others. They learn about how people from different cultures communicate. . . . And then with all those tools, we bring them together over a challenging issue."

One of the trainees was Monique Grover, a psychology major at UCSD. Since becoming a dialogue ambassador, she has conducted circle discussions on issues such as gun violence, Islamophobia, and mindfulness. Each time, about 10–20 participants have gathered to share their perspectives and listen intently to whoever possesses the talking piece as it goes around the circle.

"Our goal is mostly focused around community-building," she said. "It's focused around getting people together to strengthen those ties that they probably have but would have not otherwise known unless they got into a conversation with each other."

Grover's role in the discussion is to apply a light touch by pointing out "commonalities" in the group. "Our job at the end is to do something very simple and that's just to acknowledge that so many people had a common thread in between their conversations," she said. "It's really amazing because once we point it out, people in the room actually feel it. They're like, 'Oh, yeah, that's true, I did connect with that person in a way that I didn't think about.'"

Nobody's flawless, she said. But her aspiration is to use inclusive language to help others see that their voices and experiences matter. "Really our goal is to learn how to use language in a restorative manner, which means we offer a lot of support and a lot of accountability," she said. "These are things that I'm personally still working on."

Often it's simply enough to start the conversation and take a step back as it unfolds, she said. "It's more about giving the space than it is taking the space," Grover said. "My perspective about having conversations in general has shifted from being about me laying it all on the table and making comments and hoping someone will respond – it's shifted from doing that to more or less just asking the questions and then letting other people lay what it is they have to lay on the table."

Enabling others to feel that they are being listened to provides a "sense of comfort, a sense of support, but also a sense of empowerment," she said. "Sometimes it's so always about us that we're not willing to take a second to stop and listen to the other person."

One issue NCRC has emphasized with students is how to handle the ramifications of free speech, which is roiling college campuses. According to a poll by the Knight Foundation and Gallup, 37 percent of American college students believe it's sometimes or always acceptable to shout down a speaker they don't like or to try to prevent them from speaking in the first place, while 39 percent say it's always or sometimes acceptable to deny the press the right to cover a protest or rally on campus.[11] "Once the kids have gone through this training, they have a dialogue around talking about freedom of speech, what that means, and why it's important or not important to have people come onto the campus if you don't share their perspectives," Dinkin said.

Grover, the student dialogue ambassador, ran a circle discussion process about free speech versus hate speech after a campus speaker discussed the nature of the two and how they are often intertwined. That process is a "tool for them to think about, 'How do I engage and show respect to other people's points of view and also be able to express mine and be more inclusive in the way I talk to people?'" Maxwell said. "So we've had a lot of success with students saying this feels better to them than what they had been doing, which was basically aggressively calling people out when people make mistakes or say something they don't like."

·✦✦✦✦·

College isn't the only place where political consternation is causing significant disruption, of course. It's also increasingly becoming a problem in the American workplace. Since the 2016 presidential election, a growing number of employers "are having trouble with political divisiveness at work," Maxwell said.

For example, one major company – which she declined to name, except to call it an employer that tends to attract mostly liberal workers – approached NCRC for help after several long-term employees resigned because they had been harassed by colleagues for casting politically conservative votes. The employees "felt bullied by their coworkers for the candidate they had supported," Maxwell said. So the employer "had us come in to do workshops for everybody on their staff so they could communicate more respectfully with each other around issues that were sensitive because they didn't want to lose more people."

Sometimes, solving even the most endemic conflicts starts from the simplest of places. "Even though people come in from different backgrounds, we often begin the discussion by coming up with some type of icebreaker or common topic so that you can show that there's some common ground – just to build a little bit of momentum," Dinkin said.

Find something seemingly inconsequential that you have in common, and build from there. Chat about a TV show you both like. Bond over your mutual dislike of your favorite team's archnemesis. Reminisce about a shared toy from your youth. "And then if people are frustrated or have differences, we create a space where they can express those frustrations," Dinkin said. "It's important that people have the opportunity to vent their frustration before problem solving. So we create a space for them to do that."

The common thread tying together NCRC's various initiatives is an emphasis on teaching people how to listen to each other respectfully. When NCRC conducts a workshop, moderators often ask participants to get into pairs or groups to talk about conflicts they've personally experienced.

"We spend a lot of time on how do we show people we're listening, what skills can be used in listening, and really trying to hear what's important to people rather than just reacting," Maxwell said.

From a practical point of view, the best way to demonstrate that you're listening in the midst of conflict is "to summarize what the other person said before they state their own point of view so that people feel they're being heard," Dinkin said. "That defuses the situation and allows them to move forward toward problem-solving."

But to help people understand the importance of listening, it helps to first grasp the feeling of being ignored. So to simulate that sensation, NCRC designed an exercise in which a room of participants is split in half. One half exits the room, while the other half stays. The people left in the room are told to alternate between actively listening and not actively listening when the others come back into the room.

"And then we discuss, 'Well, how did that make you feel? What were some of the signs that they weren't listening?'" Dinkin said. For the active listeners in the exercise, "what are some of the skills that they use when they're asking probing questions? They're engaged with their body language. And how did that feel?"

Listening helps people care about each other, regardless of their differences, Maxwell said. "We're certainly groomed in our culture to not have that approach," she said. "But I would say that I can always help people see the possibility for common ground. We all kind of know inside of us that to work well with other human beings, finding common ground is the best way."

After sharing with each other, participants in NCRC mediation training sessions often remark about how empowered they feel. "It feels really good when someone listens to you," Maxwell said.

Bridge builders recognize that active listening goes hand in hand with empathy. Without it, conflict resolution is nearly impossible. By learning how to listen intently to each other, people often get better at identifying with each other's perspectives, even if they continue to disagree. "Most people have empathy – they just don't know how to show it," Maxwell said.

For example, she recounted an episode in which she consulted with a leader about how to handle conflict in her workplace. The executive was frustrated that her employees disliked her approach. "Her natural response, which is very common in this culture, is to immediately figure out how to solve the problem," Maxwell said. "And she means it with the best intentions possible." But her employees were never satisfied, the woman relayed to Maxwell. "I just don't know what to do, and I'm at my wit's end," the leader told the NCRC Training Institute director.

What Maxwell identified was that the leader's staff members were "emotionally expressive" in their discussions about conflict. "And when you just try to solve the problem immediately, they don't feel like you're showing any empathy, even if you believe you are," Maxwell told the executive.

She counseled the leader to change her entire approach to conversations with her employees. Rather than immediately seeking to fix things, she should simply acknowledge their feelings and paraphrase their comments in response to them before going into problem-solving mode. "That changed everything," Maxwell said. "It completely changed her relationship. They even thanked her and said they felt like she finally got it. And all she did was add something that wasn't natural to her but that they needed."

In some sessions, NCRC trainers promote a process called ART. The "A" requires listeners to be actively aware of their companions' feelings. "Because in order to respond in a way that's thoughtful, I have to be mindful about my interactions with other humans," Maxwell said. The "R" requires listeners to be respectful. "How do we show we're listening? How do we ask questions? How do we show we're engaging with the other person? That's responding respectively," she said. And the "T" requires listeners to troubleshoot together with the speakers. "And that means how do we share our own perspective? How do we look at what's important to each person?"

As veteran professionals in the world of conflict resolution, Dinkin and Maxwell have observed how the failure to respectfully acknowledge each other's perspectives is often the root cause of division. Bridge builders recognize that they can't span a gap unless they have an accurate understanding of what's on the other side.

"In a typical negotiation, where it really breaks down is where you have two people who are in a dispute, and they can't get the matter resolved themselves because they're not hearing each other," Dinkin said. "What happens is that someone will say something, the other person interrupts, and then the conversation just escalates and gets louder and louder because they are just trying to talk over each other. So the negotiation or the discussion often fails."

That's why engaging in the act of perspective-taking is crucial before any problem-solving efforts can succeed. Participants in the conflict need to demonstrate that they have "a clear understanding of each person's perspective before we start trying to negotiate what can we do about it," Maxwell said.

When people acknowledge and contemplate each other's perspectives in the midst of conflict, they often begin to realize that their preconceptions about their opponent's background, reasoning, or motives were skewed.

"'Oh, *that's* why you did that. I assumed *this*,'" Maxwell said, quoting the people she counsels through conflict. "Or, 'I thought it was because of *this*.' [There's] a lot of clarification and understanding building. And then we're able to negotiate based on interests rather than their position. It's a process that I lead them through to help them to have more empathy and understanding and to be heard for maybe the first time."

That doesn't necessarily mean they need to agree on all the facts pertaining to their conflict. Although it would certainly make things easier and it's something we should strive for, the reality is that resolving conflict does not require people to agree on everything related to the truth.

"In our interactions with one another about something that happened between us, there are some irrefutable facts, but there is a lot more that is perspective and our view of the world and how we experience the situation," Maxwell said. "So we work a lot on helping people understand each person's view of the world and their own perspective and their own truth, if you will. That's not to say that factual truths aren't important, too. But where we get hiccups is the perception, more than the facts, in personal relations."

Like others I interviewed for this book, I asked the NCRC leaders how we can prevent compromise from going extinct. I figured that professional mediators, of all people, would wholeheartedly promote the concept of compromise.

I was wrong. Sort of. They would prefer to redefine the essence of compromise.

"It's limiting to think in terms of only compromise," Maxwell said. "Certainly, in some things there has to be some sort of compromise – especially around financial issues. But so many times people will come in with a conflict when I'm helping them resolve it, and they think they have to go 50 percent, but we are able to come up with new ideas."

Instead of viewing the universe of solutions as finite, bridge builders help people recalibrate their approach. Telling someone they have to give something up may make them feel defensive or defeated. But approaching the situation with the perspective that each person can walk away relatively satisfied paves the way for dynamic solutions. It comes down to helping people see their circumstances – and see others – differently.

"It's expanding the pie," Dinkin said. "You don't have to cut the pie in half and say you each get one piece. The idea is that if you have the opportunity to have the dialogue and are creative in your brainstorming and come up with a range of solutions, you might end up with six pieces. And then, rather than each just [getting one], you each get three."

The key is to "broaden the conversation to find out what's important to each person and why it's important," Maxwell said. "It's how do we mutually gain, rather than feeling [like] I have to give things up. It's a natural human response to be resistant to giving things up. But through understanding and dialogue, you'll see it differently and expand the pie and look at more options, rather than fewer."

Many people come into conflict from "extreme ends," she acknowledged. "But there's a lot of people in the middle, and they just need to bring out the good that's in them. The willingness to hear each other is going to be there. I just find it to be true in basically every workshop I do. People have that within them."

Conclusion

We'll have to agree to disagree.

It's one of those clichés most of us have used at some point. After arguing, we acknowledge we're not going to change each other's mind, but we need to move on from the debate because our relationship is more important. We still care about each other.

That cliché is in danger of becoming an anachronism. In our polarized age, many of us refuse to even associate with people who think differently, look differently, act differently, or pray differently. And when we do choose to interact with others who aren't like us, it's more of a confrontation than a conversation. We quickly devolve into invective and intolerance.

And we're quick on the draw, too. In our call-out culture, we fire off social media screeds blasting others for their misbegotten choice of words or personal failures. We'd rather embarrass people on the other side than form meaningful relationships with them. It gets us precisely nowhere. That doesn't mean we shouldn't call out injustices. Of course we should. But the manner in which we do so and the mechanisms through which we do so represent the difference between relationships that deepen stagnation and relationships that generate substantive change.

We have a choice to make. We can accept our crisis of

affective polarization as unchangeable, or we can reject
the status quo and pursue relationships, conversation,
and understanding with people of difference in hopes of
achieving meaningful and lasting transformation. This
is the very essence of bridge building.

The fiber of our democracy is in desperate need of
bridge builders who refuse to concede that affective
polarization is our permanent reality. Even our health
and wellbeing are at stake. If anything has shown us
the urgency of bridge building, it's the COVID-19 pandemic. You may not like your neighbors, but surely you
don't want them to die. And yet the pandemic has illus-
trated that the forces of polarization are so powerful
that they can, in fact, kill us.

Bridge builders recognize that no matter how wide
the divide between themselves and people across the
ravine, both sides will be better off when the gap has
been spanned. Like the people they are trying to bring
together, bridge builders come from different walks
of life. They may even vehemently disagree with each
other. But despite their personal, political, and cultural
differences, they share many of the same qualities and
strategies. They handle their construction projects, if
you will, with a similar blueprint.

Here are five keys to being a bridge builder, based
on the experiences of the people I interviewed for this
book:

1. *Acknowledge the past, educate others about it, and
refuse to idealize it.*
Bridge builders don't ignore events that have led to
conflict, pain, and exclusion. They acknowledge what
happened in the past. They teach people about it. They
validate emotional responses to old hurts.

Bridge builders believe in accountability. But they
also believe that dwelling on blame triggers a counterproductive knee-jerk response or leads to shame, which

foils their goal of pursuing healing and cooperation for the sake of advancing social dignity, interconnectedness, and policy transformation.

2. *Don't label people.*

Yes, there are Republicans and Democrats, White people and Black people, urban dwellers and rural residents, upper-class people and working-class people, citizens and immigrants without legal documentation – and everything in between. Bridge builders recognize those distinctions. They are not color-blind. They are not ignorant of ignorance. But they see people of difference differently. Where the rest of us see shallowness, they see depth. Where the rest of us see homogeneity, they see heterogeneity.

When we label people, we burden them with our assumptions, and they are less likely to consider our perspectives and engage with us in problem-solving. Bridge builders believe that love resides in the hearts of people who aren't like them. And they believe that loved people love people. Just ask Azar Maluki of the Iraqi and American Reconciliation Project.

To be clear, their views of others in the midst of conflict are often aspirational. But they believe that labels are counterproductive in that they perpetuate harmful stereotypes and foster hostility, as Irshad Manji articulated in her 2019 book, *Don't Label Me.*

Bridge builders see personal flaws and bad behavior in others. But they believe that people must be inspired to change and challenged to change, not berated to change. There's a big difference.

3. *Embrace conflict.*

Bridge builders recognize that we don't need to agree on everything to come alongside each other in authentic relationships. Eboo Patel, the founder of the Interfaith Youth Core, put it succinctly: "How do you have a diverse democracy if the only way you can work together is to agree on everything?"

You can't. Bridge builders can agree to disagree and still reach a better understanding of each other that leads to cooperation. They recognize that conflict is a natural part of the human experience. In fact, it can lead to genuine personal connections when managed delicately.

"We're not trying to do away with conflict," said David Blankenhorn, cofounder and president of Braver Angels. "Most progress would not have occurred without conflict. The only way you get rid of conflict is to get rid of freedom. Free people disagree, often passionately, and that's normal and healthy. The question is, how do you deal with it?"

Bridge builders deal with it by choosing inclusion over exclusion. They choose their words carefully, believing that the language of inclusivity nudges others to confront their own intolerance, hate, and unconscious biases.

Bridge builders recognize that conflict doesn't need to devolve into bitterness. "We don't have to have the same perspective. We don't have to believe the same things. I can still see you as a human being," said Jodie Geddes, president of Coming to the Table's advisory board. "For me, the conversations that have been really enriching are the ones that conflict has been at the center."

4. *Listen when most people would talk.*
This sounds like the opposite of the prior point. But healthy disagreement can't occur unless you first listen to the other side. That way you can truly absorb what others are saying.

Bridge builders recognize that unless people feel heard, they won't engage. But choosing to listen requires an attitude of humility that's very rare. And yet that quality is common among bridge builders. They know that they have shortcomings, too. Which should give us all the confidence to admit our own weaknesses.

Just ask Monique Grover, the UCSD student who was trained as a dialogue ambassador through the National Conflict Resolution Center. She makes a point of listening to others who aren't like her talk about their life experiences and perspectives – not just because they deserve to be heard but because she needs to hear them. "When I hear their stories, it really makes you sit and think how I perceived them before I met them," she said. "When I take a second and I reflect on how my perception of them has changed, my perception of myself and how I look at the world and how I view other people has really changed."

Bridge builders approach life from an inquisitive posture because they understand that there are things they don't know about the world – and the people – around them. They cultivate a mentality of curiosity. They are always looking to broaden their perspectives on life. In a way, bridge building requires continuous education.

"If I really don't understand what you're saying, I wonder how it is that you have come to the space that you're in," said Tom DeWolf, cofounder of Coming to the Table. "That requires me to know you and know your background and know your family, your connections, your history. It involves wonder. It involves curiosity. It involves imagination."

On a basic human level, listening involves a degree of humility because it requires you to temporarily set aside your own opinions to invest in the person who is speaking, even when the other person is clearly wrong. But bridge builders are willing to take the first step. They recognize that people can't become grace givers until they first receive grace. Then they'll be much more likely to listen during difficult conversations when it's time for bridge builders to share hard truths.

5. Recognize that dialogue isn't always enough to change hearts.

Bridge builders understand that sometimes you need to find alternative ways of connecting with others because certain people won't engage in meaningful conversation no matter how much effort you make.

So bridge builders use a wide range of media to deliver messages, like artwork or performances, which the Iraqi and American Reconciliation Project has used successfully. Or they use social media, like the Everyday Projects, to connect people from completely different cultures in a demonstration of their shared humanity.

Ultimately, bridge builders recognize that strategically selecting the medium is critical to delivering the message. Without careful attention to the method of communication and the approach to relationship building, attempts to span the gap will falter.

While bridge builders are often successful at bringing people together on a small scale, the natural question is, how do we translate their connective techniques into a national movement? After all, the forces of polarization seem to be worsening. President Joe Biden may do all he can to fight these forces – and he certainly has an opportunity to exemplify big-tent leadership, fostering coalitions and compromises that achieve progress for the sake of the common good. He has repeatedly pledged to be a president for all Americans, not just those who voted for him. But he faces deeply ingrained opposition – in the Republican Party, from progressive Democrats who disapprove of compromise, and in the form of human nature, technological trends, and the open wounds of history. The grouping effect in our society and our politics, which manifests itself in government gridlock, poses a grave threat to our democracy under Biden or any other leader. The explosion of misinformation has added considerable fuel to the fire, weakening the connection between Americans and authentic journalism. Powerful new digital gatekeepers have seized control of people's news consumption habits, leading users to distrust legitimate news reports and spread falsehoods that weaken the few bridges we have left.

These forces cannot be overcome with a clever tweet, a wicked zinger on cable news, or even with the top-down imposition of new policies. They cannot be overcome with an inspiring speech or a political donation. It will take something much more time-consuming and difficult to achieve. It will take the development of authentic relationships between people of difference. These dynamic personal relationships – which spawn the type of effective conversation that leads to deep contemplation and then to action – are the fundamental pursuit of virtually everyone I interviewed for this book. They are the key to thwarting affective polarization – the basic ingredient in the recipe for change.

It sounds simple, but it's not. Not at all. It's terribly difficult because our natural human inclination is to band together with people like us. It's how we're genetically wired. We'd rather stay within our comfort zone than reach out to people of difference. But establishing those human connections is precisely what we need to cure the disease of tribalism that afflicts our nation.

In politics, we need to implement processes and structures that force legislators to interact with each other outside and inside their legislative chambers. In media, we need to invest in on-the-ground nonprofit journalism that involves reporters building relationships with citizens in their communities. In social media, we need to leverage all-powerful algorithms to spread grassroots friend-to-friend fact-checking rooted in sound journalism, and we need the major platforms to promote cross-cultural connections instead of private groups and crackpot content that encourage hate and isolation.

When it comes to race, what we saw in the wake of George Floyd's killing was an organic movement in which many White Americans began to recognize their inherent privilege for the first time and began to join Black people in demanding change. But we need to go much further than street protests. The noticeably diverse uprising throughout America was, I hope, a catalyst for the formation of serious relationships between people of difference. Those relationships are the key that will unlock political and social progress on systemic inequities. If the White people who rose up in outrage truly want to usher in long-lasting change, they'll begin to invest their time and energy in getting to know, and care about, Black Americans who have been oppressed for centuries. After all, as Tom DeWolf said in Chapter 1, coming to the table is not that difficult. It's staying at the table that's challenging.

I'm not naive enough to think that this is straightforward. In politics, we'll still have powerful party leaders who pressure their members to resist compromise. In law enforcement, we'll still have violent and racist police. In media, we'll still have sensational stories lacking the type of nuance that generates trust between journalists and the public. In social media, we'll still have to deal with the downsides of profit-focused algorithms and their tendency to exacerbate confirmation bias. And we can and should continue to confront the forces of polarization.

But we can't argue our way out of this. Simply presenting the facts is not enough to change people's minds. Spewing hot takes is of little value, too. We can opine about the things that make us mad and proclaim that policy change is the answer. That's pretty easy, actually. It's much simpler to change laws than it is to change minds. Don't get me wrong – we need to change laws.

But if people don't care enough about each other, lasting change will remain evasive. The way to fell the pillars of polarization is to promote individual interaction and cultivate understanding through personal relationships, which form the basis of our society. Because when that occurs, people will begin to change things on their own.

For the most part, the bridge builders I interviewed for this book are pursuing change organically. Yet the lessons from their experiences can be applied on a broader scale. Here are several things we can do to pursue togetherness from a national perspective – all predicated on integrating a culture of relationship-building into the institutions that drive our politics, education, and daily lives:

1. *Encourage a national service movement.*
Have you ever noticed how it's easier to have a difficult conversation with someone while taking a walk together than while facing each other in a confrontational posture? Similarly, one of the best ways for people from different backgrounds to bridge their differences is to come together shoulder to shoulder, rather than face to face. Genuine relationships are formed when people are serving others together. The actual project may not even matter much. But in a collaborative atmosphere, conversations begin to happen, minds start to change, and common ground is forged.

That's why it's critical for bridge builders to be intentional about creating spaces that promote cooperation and public service through organizations such as non-profits, schools, governments, and religious institutions. Those spaces of cooperation cultivate an appreciation of differences, which greases the gears of a healthy democracy. When you're helping others, you're more likely to see your fellow helpers as allies – and you're more likely to empathize with and understand the people you're assisting.

Patel's Interfaith Youth Core focuses much of its bridge building work on the promotion of public service projects involving volunteers from a wide range of backgrounds. "Isn't there something really remarkable about a society in which people can disagree on some fundamental things and work together on other fundamental things?" Patel said.

But we can do this on a much larger scale.

The framework for a national service movement is already in place. In 2009, President Barack Obama signed bipartisan legislation nearly quadrupling the number of national service positions, through groups such as AmeriCorps and the Peace Corps, from 65,000 to 250,000. But funding to make that increase a reality has not materialized. And yet, interest in national public service programs remains high. In the decade after the legislation's passage, the number of public service applications topped AmeriCorps positions by a ratio of anywhere from three-to-one to five-to-one, according to a Brookings Institution study.[1]

In March 2020, the National Commission on Military, National, and Public Service published a report calling for one million federally funded national public service positions by 2031, the seventieth anniversary of President John F. Kennedy's plea to the American people: "Ask not what your country can do for you – ask what you can do for your country." The report called for service opportunities to be better marketed and offered to a broad range of people from different backgrounds, including unemployed youth, people living with disabilities, and people who are reintegrating into society after serving time in prison.[2]

William Galston, who was involved in the creation of AmeriCorps as a domestic policy adviser to President Bill Clinton, said public service has a uniquely unifying effect on its participants. "For 100 years, reformers have been looking for the moral equivalent of war," said

Galston, who also cofounded bipartisanship promoter No Labels. Public service is the "civilian equivalent of military experience, where the [service opportunity] is the equivalent of the foxhole – the platoon that you're all in together with a common mission despite your differences."

There are also significant practical benefits of an increase in national service. Among AmeriCorps alumni, for example, 80 percent say the program made them "more likely to attain a college degree, vote, volunteer, care about community problems, and know how to effect practical solutions to such problems," according to the Brookings study.[3]

Brookings fellow Isabel Sawhill and John Bridgeland, vice chairman of the Service Year Alliance and a former director of the White House Domestic Policy Council under President George W. Bush, wrote that a voluntary "universal national service" program would "build bridges instead of walls, limiting toxic tribalism and social division." They estimated that Congress could accommodate an additional quarter million Americans with an annual allocation of about $5 billion.[4] That's less than 0.1 percent of federal spending in the 2020 fiscal year.[5]

"National service has clear benefits," Sawhill and Bridgeland argued in the *Washington Post*. "It changes the young people who participate, giving them new skills and a clearer path to college and career. It helps communities, providing extra hands for dealing with natural disasters, tutoring students, or improving the environment. Perhaps its greatest benefit is reducing the social distance between 'us' and 'them' by creating opportunities for people from different backgrounds to work together."

They also suggested that the country create what they called an American Exchange Program, in which families would volunteer to "host young people during their year of service after being matched through an online platform." The American Exchange Program would be designed to foster "greater understanding" between Americans from blue states and red states, cities and rural areas, and across other divides.[6]

2. Teach students techniques for effective engagement, promote collaboration, and improve class history lessons.

Though I believe there's still time for adults to bridge their divides, let's suppose for a moment that there's no hope for them. If that's the case, we can at least agree that there's still hope for our kids.

They may have absorbed certain stereotypes, just as the *Everyday Africa* founders discovered, but in many ways, students are still forming their habits and opinions about life and each other. Though diversity and inclusion are often discussed as important principles in schools, they're not often taught in a practical sense. While experts widely agree that peer-to-peer learning can be a powerful component of the educational experience, kids rarely work together with students who aren't like them, in part due to the fact that our schools are politically, racially, and socioeconomically segregated, albeit legally so. We should be teaching kids how to engage with people of difference, but these lessons need to go far beyond classroom lectures.

Students also need to be forced to forge working relationships with their contemporaries within the classroom and even from other schools. In the era of live video conferencing and remote schooling, which took off out of necessity during the height of the pandemic, there's no longer any excuse for allowing students to stay ensconced in the comfortable confines of their school buildings. Field trips aren't necessary to learn what the world is really like. We should encourage teachers to collaborate with fellow teachers in other school districts to pair students together on class projects that will expose them to political, cultural, racial, and socioeconomic diversity. Yes, friction is inevitable. But that's precisely what we need – because allowing students to grow up in a bubble without getting to know others who aren't like them is a recipe for greater division later in life.

What's more, schools need to reexamine their textbooks and coursework to ensure that students are learning the full scope of history on divisive topics such as racism and inequity. Be the Bridge founder Latasha Morrison noted that schools aren't teaching kids enough about, for example, America's history of redlining – the practice of blocking people of color from White neighborhoods – or its history of racism against Indigenous Americans or its history of discrimination in the military or its history of police brutality. "We have intentionally kept people ignorant in our country," she said. "When you don't know better, it's impossible for people to do better."

3. Nudge college students to build connections with other students who aren't like them.
College is becoming a place where students congregate mostly with people who are like them and believe the same things as them, rather than a place that promotes the free exchange of ideas and lasting relationships with people of difference. With the rise of social media, it has become exceedingly easy and, in fact, common for incoming college students to select their fellow first-year dormitory roommates long before arriving on campus. It's like online dating without the romance. They can pick and choose their roommates based on what feels comfortable to them. For example, they can weed out prospective dormmates based on political ideology.

Don't agree on middle-class tax rates? We can't live together. It sounds ridiculous, but it's exactly what's

happening. And it's counterproductive if our hope is
for college to be a place where students are exposed to
new ways of thinking, learn how to interact with people
from different backgrounds, and form transformational
relationships that last a lifetime. At the University of
Virginia, for example, about 65 percent of first-year
students pick their roommates in advance.[7]

But some universities are beginning to recognize
that allowing students to pick their own roommates is
contributing to the grouping effect that solidifies our
polarized culture. At Duke University, for example,
leaders reported in 2017 that nearly half of students
were choosing their own roommates before arriving
on campus – and that most of those who did so came
from wealthy families. "It was basically the well-off
students finding each other," one administrator told the
Washington Post.[8]

So in 2018, Duke announced that it would begin assigning freshman roommates at random. Administrators do
take into account certain lifestyle factors, such as sleep
schedules and study habits, to ensure pairings aren't
unnecessarily awkward.[9] (If there's one divide that can
never be bridged, it's the gap between morning people
and night people.) But for the most part, students
are paired with someone they don't know – someone
whose life experiences, political background, race, religion, or socioeconomic status may be quite different.
A few years before Duke made the change, New York
University began pairing students with roommates from
different ZIP codes, often with an eye toward promoting relationships between students who aren't from the
same country.[10] At Bowdoin College in Maine, first-year
students are intentionally paired with roommates from
different backgrounds. The college won't even allow
student athletes to room together, believing that it's
critical to teach students how to handle conflict with
each other.[11]

The hope is that random pairings will foster dialogue and understanding over time. And if research
is any indication, it will. A study by David R.
Harris, former president of Union College and provost of Tufts
University, determined that White "roommates who
were paired with students of color became more open-
minded about race."[12]

**4. *Foster relationships on Capitol Hill by overhauling
congressional rules and procedures.***
Much has been written and said in recent decades about
the disappearance of relationships and comity among
Republicans and Democrats on Capitol Hill. Gone are
the days when they would have drinks with each other
after debating legislation, and gone are the days when
their kids socialized, we are often told. It's almost comi-
cal to think about Republicans and Democrats hanging
out in Washington. These days, members jet home
for the weekend as soon as the congressional schedule
wraps up. And they fly back with moments to spare
before it kicks up again the following week. Lacking
relationships with each other, legislators are naturally
inclined to care little about each other's perspectives.

"The schedule is part of the problem," Galston said.
"It's part of the problem not only because it encourages
polarization but because it discourages deliberation.
You're running from one place to another, and you
don't even get a chance to develop working relationships with members of your own committee, let alone
the other party."

It's hard enough for lawmakers to justify working
with each other when the political system is set up to
reward party loyalty. There's too much for them to lose
– their internal party influence, their funders, and even
their seats. But it would be at least a little harder for
them to blatantly spurn each other if they had genuine
personal relationships once again.

Other behind-the-scenes elements of process that might seem arcane have also stoked the flames of division on Capitol Hill in ways outsiders can't see. "Even the shuttle buses at orientation for freshman members of Congress are divided between Republicans and Democrats," Jason Grumet, president of the Bipartisan Policy Center, said in written testimony submitted to the US House Select Committee on the Modernization of Congress. "Caucus meetings and policy lunches are conducted along purely partisan lines. Congressional committees, which traditionally have been engines of democracy and the place where members work together to build bipartisan bridges, have been systematically weakened as party leaders increasingly script and dictate major pieces of legislation."[13]

The Bipartisan Policy Center's Commission on Political Reform proposed several practical changes on Capitol Hill to foster relationships between people on both sides of the aisle. They include adopting a full five-day workweek for several consecutive weeks to disincentivize traveling home for long weekends and then giving members a full week off so they can go and meet with constituents; encouraging bipartisan fact-finding trips, such as the one that Bob Inglis took to Australia, where he changed his mind on climate change; taking steps to depoliticize the membership orientation process by removing party leadership elections from the proceedings; and creating ways to promote relationships between staff members from both parties.[14]

Encouragingly, the seeds of bipartisanship have been planted despite the political weeds that usually constrict collaboration on Capitol Hill. In 2017, No Labels successfully promoted the formation of the Problem Solvers Caucus – a cohort of about four dozen members of Congress, split equally among Republicans and Democrats, who are committed to pursuing bipartisan legislation. The group has since played a crucial role in the passage of criminal justice reform, an overhaul of House rules, and school safety legislation. The Problem Solvers Caucus has also backed proposals to reduce healthcare costs, including slashing the price of prescription drugs, and proposals to invest in the nation's infrastructure.[15] (Yes, that's right – the Problem Solvers Caucus is trying to build literal bridges. Go figure.)

But before the group even got started, its members took time to form relationships with each other outside the spotlight. "They spent the first 18 months of their existence in the very human activity of breaking bread together and developing a modicum of trust. And that was part of a very deliberate strategy," Galston said. "We didn't think that they could start to address serious policy issues until they were ready for it – and we didn't think they would be ready until [there was] trust that had been built up to work with people on the other side of the aisle and not be stabbed in the back by them."

Quite simply, relationships matter – just as much, if not more so, on Capitol Hill as anywhere else. "That elementary human truth applies at the political level and not just in civil society," Galston said.

I suppose it's appropriate that I began working on this book in earnest during the longest federal government shutdown in US history in late 2018. Remember that? Events of that magnitude would be generation-defining in past political eras, but for us, it was pretty normal – and ultimately even forgettable, given what happened next. In that case, to refresh your memory, politicians on both sides of the aisle couldn't agree on how to fund the government for 35 days because of their bitter clash over President Trump's proposal to build a wall – a physical embodiment of division – on the border with Mexico.[16] That's where our polarized politics led us: to a paralyzing debate over installing the opposite of a bridge between us and people we perceive as different from us.

In the midst of the government shutdown, my wife and I took a Metro ride to downtown Washington, DC. From there, we walked a few blocks toward The Ellipse, a park just south of the White House, to see the National Christmas Tree. Little did we know, the tree lights had been turned off due to the government shutdown.

Yes, Christmas was canceled in 2018 because of Washington's failure to bridge its divides. It reminded me of that moment in the 1964 TV special *Rudolph the Red-Nosed Reindeer* when Santa declares that Christmas is canceled because of thick fog.

What better analogy for our polarized culture? We are blinded by the fog of our differences. And the only way we can navigate through it is by realizing that we all have a part to play in lighting the way, just as the closed-minded Santa realized he couldn't fly his sleigh without Rudolph.

In the time since that canceled Christmas, the nation has gone through the impeachment and acquittal of a president, the explosion of a polarizing pandemic, the eruption of tension over race, and the election of Biden as the 46th President following a bitter campaign in which the incumbent falsely attacked the outcome as fraudulent, leading to a Capitol insurrection, another presidential impeachment, and another acquittal as this book was going to press. These polarizing events will soon be succeeded by additional polarizing events – and we, as a dysfunctional family of a nation, will continue down a path toward a state of irreconcilable differences that threatens to hobble our democracy, our economy, and our personal wellbeing unless we fight back against the forces that perpetually seek to divide us.

"United there is little we cannot do in a host of cooperative ventures," Kennedy said during his inaugural address, calling on the nation to "eradicate disease,"

stimulate the economy, and pursue global peace –
endeavors that are still relevant today. "Divided there is
little we can do – for we dare not meet a powerful challenge at odds and split asunder."[17]

To be sure, we need so much more than bridge building to address our many challenges. But the journey
toward substantive change starts with tackling our political, racial, economic, religious, and cultural schisms
on a personal level. And the only way to do that – the
only way to curb our crisis of tribalism – is by cultivating authentic relationships and conversations between
people of difference and then using those dynamic connections to bring about change. This is what we must do
if we want "the better angels of our nature" to prevail,
as President Abraham Lincoln famously put it on the
eve of the Civil War.[18]

"It's not like we haven't gone through these times
before – growing diversity, growing polarization," Eboo
Patel reminded me. "Americans, over the course of time,
have enlarged the circle of inclusion and bridged divides
within it – and that's what we need now."

Let's start building.

Acknowledgments

If you're anything like me, you've faced discouragement from time to time due to the culture of polarization that surrounds us. You're sick of the fighting. That makes two of us.

And, let's be honest, journalists like me often contribute to the culture of divisiveness.

I figured it was time for a different approach. That's why I sought out the bridge builders you met in this book – because we can all learn from them in one way or another. So I'd like to thank them for believing in their respective missions and for sharing their stories with me.

I'm indebted to my editor, Louise Knight, for giving me the opportunity to tell these stories. Louise embraced the vision for this book from the very beginning, and I'm grateful to her for helping me refine this concept and bring it to life. As I joked with Louise, you can't write a book that emphasizes the importance of listening and then not listen to your editor's suggestions. This book is vastly better for her guidance and expertise. Copy-editor Sarah Dancy made this manuscript shine with her exceptional eye for detail. I was also fortunate to have the assistance of many other brilliant folks at Polity, including Inès Boxman, Neil de Cort, and Rachel Moore. Their contributions were essential to the final product.

I'd also like to thank my current and former colleagues, editors, and leaders at *USA Today* and Gannett for supporting me throughout this process, including Maribel Perez Wadsworth, Amalie Nash, Nicole Carroll, Jeff Taylor, Philana Patterson, David Brinkerhoff, and Michelle Maltais. I'm grateful to have work at a news organization that is still investing in journalism despite the trying times for our industry.

I'd also like to thank my friend (as well as two-time *Jeopardy!* champion and *Wheel of Fortune* champion) Jason Idalski for his assistance in copyediting before I turned in my manuscript. Thank you also to my friend Caleb Cohen for his help with my website, NathanBomey.com.

I'm incredibly blessed to have the support of my family, including my parents, Deanna and Randy Bomey, my brother, Dan Bomey, and my in-laws, Lynn and Ben Blazier.

And, finally, I am forever grateful to my wife, Kathryn Bomey, for her encouragement, love, and support throughout this process. It also doesn't hurt that she's an exceptional writer and editor herself. If you're ever going to write a book, I recommend marrying for love first and a good editor second.

Interviews

Unless otherwise referenced in the endnotes, the quotes and facts in this book came from these personal interviews:

Alan Miller – June 26, 2020
Alex Mahadevan – June 16, 2020
Alexa Volland – June 16, 2020
Alvin Edwards – January 31, 2019
Atorod Azizinamini – April 15, 2020
Austin Merrill – March 13, 2019
Azar Maluki – March 1, 2019
Bill Doherty – March 25, 2020
Bob Inglis – January 17, 2019
Brenda Brown-Grooms – January 31, 2019
Dana Coester – February 18, 2019
David Blankenhorn – April 15, 2020
Eboo Patel – March 20, 2019
Gina Dahlia – February 18, 2019
Heaven Taylor-Wynn – June 16, 2020
Jane Carrigan – January 21, 2019
Jessica Belt Saem Eldahr – March 1, 2019
Jodie Geddes – February 10, 2019, and June 12, 2020
John Walsh – January 14, 2019
Jonathan Rauch – March 17, 2020
Joseph Lichterman – February 26, 2019

Kathy McKay – March 1, 2019
Katy Byron – June 16, 2020
Kristyn Wellesley – June 16, 2020
Latasha Morrison – March 27, 2020
Lisa Maxwell – February 18, 2019
Mary Lambert – March 6, 2019
Michael Cheuk – January 31, 2019
Monique Grover – March 20, 2019
Nancy Andrews – February 18, 2019
Peter DiCampo – April 1, 2020
Pinar Okumus – April 10, 2020
Rabia Povich – January 31, 2019
Sami Rasouli – March 26, 2020
Sam Wineburg – June 14, 2020
Scott Heron – March 26, 2020
Steven Dinkin – February 18, 2019
Thomas Stallworth III – January 14, 2019
Tom DeWolf – February 10, 2019, and June 12, 2020
Tom Gutherz – January 31, 2019
William Galston – January 8, 2020
Zoshia Minto – March 23, 2019

Notes

Introduction

1 Gabriel Sanchez and Edward Vargas, "73% of Democrats Are Wearing Masks to Fight Coronavirus. Only 59% of Republicans Are," *Washington Post*, May 15, 2020, https://www.washingtonpost.com/politics/2020/05/15/73-democrats-are-wearing-mas ks-fight-coronavirus-only-59-republicans-are/.

2 Michael Scherer, "Trump's Mockery of Wearing Masks Divides Republicans," *Washington Post*, May 27, 2020, https://www.washingtonpost.com/politics/trumps-mockery-of-wearing-masks-divides-republicans/2020/05/26/2c2bdc02-9f61-11ea-81bb-c2f70f01034b_story.html.

3 Hannah Allam, "Researchers Say That The Debate Over The Coronavirus May Become More Violent," NPR, May 15, 2020, https://www.npr.org/2020/05/15/857105166/researchers-say-that-the-debate-over-the-coronavirus-may-become-mor e-violent.

4 Margaret Talev, "*Axios*-Ipsos Poll: There Is No New Normal," *Axios*, July 7, 2020, https://www.axios.com/axios-ipsos-poll-coronavirus-index-15-weeks-e4eb 53cc-9bc8-4cac-8285-07e5e5ef6b2b.html.

5 "CDC COVID Data Tracker," Centers for Disease

220

Control and Prevention, https://covid.cdc.gov/covid-data-tracker/.

6 "The Partisan Divide on Political Values Grows Even Wider," Pew Research Center, October 5, 2017, https://www.people-press.org/2017/10/05/the-partisan-divide-on-political-values-grows-even-wider/.
7 Eric Bradner, Arlette Saenz, and Sarah Mucha, "Biden Embraces Healer-in-Chief Role in Return to Campaign Trail," CNN, June 8, 2020, https://www.cnn.com/2020/06/08/politics/joe-biden-return-to-campaign-trail/index.html.
8 Sam Gringlas, Scott Neuman, and Camila Domonoske, "'Far From Over': Trump Refuses to Concede as Biden's Margin of Victory Widens," NPR, November 7, 2020, https://www.npr.org/sections/live-updates-2020-election-results/2020/11/07/932062684/far-from-over-trump-refuses-to-concede-as-ap-others-call-election-for-biden.
9 "Presidential Results," CNN, November 12, 2020, https://www.cnn.com/election/2020/results/president.
10 Glenn Kessler and Salvador Rizzo, "President Trump's False Claims of Vote Fraud: A Chronology," *Washington Post*, November 5, 2020, https://www.washingtonpost.com/politics/2020/11/05/president-trumps-false-claims-vote-fraud-chronology/.
11 Cybersecurity & Infrastructure Security Agency, "Joint Statement from Elections Infrastructure Government Coordinating Council & the Election Infrastructure Sector Coordinating Executive Committees," November 12, 2020, https://www.cisa.gov/news/2020/11/12/joint-statement-elections-infrastructure-government-coordinating-council-election.
12 Kim Hart, "Exclusive Poll: Most Democrats See Republicans As Racist, Sexist," *Axios*, November 12,

2018, https://www.axios.com/poll-democrats-and-
republicans-hate-each-other-racist-ignorant-evil-
99ae7afc-5a51-42be-8ee2-3959e43ce320.html.
13 Ibid.
14 Mary Baker, "Gartner Survey Shows 47% of
Employees Report Being Distracted at Work by
the US Presidential Election," Gartner, February
18, 2020, https://www.gartner.com/en/newsroom/
press-releases/2020-02-18-gartner-survey-shows-
47--of-employees-report-being-di.
15 Susan Page, "Divided We Fall? Americans See our
Angry Political Debate as 'A Big Problem,'" *USA
Today*, December 9, 2019, https://www.usatoday.
com/story/opinion/2019/12/05/backstory-america-
divided-how-usa-today-help/2599103001/.
16 Joan Conrow, "Anti-Vaccine Movement Embraced
at Extremes of Political Spectrum, Study Finds,"
Cornell Alliance for Science, https://alliance
forscience.cornell.edu/blog/2018/06/anti-vaccin
e-movement-embraced-extremes-political-spectrum
study-finds/.
17 Nathan Bomey, *After the Fact: The Erosion of
Truth and the Inevitable Rise of Donald Trump*,
Prometheus Books, 2018.
18 Penelope Muse Abernathy, "News Deserts and
Ghost Newspapers: Will Local News Survive?"
University of North Carolina at Chapel Hill
Hussman School of Journalism and Media, June
2020, https://www.usnewsdeserts.com/wp-content/
uploads/2020/06/2020_News_Deserts_and_Ghost_
Newspapers.pdf.
19 Tatyana Hopkins, "Social Media Companies
Profiting from Misinformation," GW Today, June
19, 2020, https://gwtoday.gwu.edu/social-media-co
mpanies-profiting-misinformation.
20 Daniel Yudkin, Stephen Hawkins, and Tim Dixon,
"The Perception Gap: How False Impressions Are

Pulling Americans Apart," More in Common, June 2019, https://perceptiongap.us/media/zaslaroc/perce ption-gap-report-1-0-3.pdf.

21 Ibid.

22 Stephen Hawkins, et al., "Hidden Tribes: A Study of America's Polarized Landscape," More in Common, 2018, https://static1.squarespace.com/ static/5a70a7c3010027736a22740f/t/5bbcea6b78 17f7bf7342b718/1539107467397/hidden_tribes_ report-2.pdf.

23 Ibid.

24 Jennifer Levitz, Erin Ailworth, and Tawnell D. Hobbs, "George Floyd and Derek Chauvin: The Lives of the Victim and His Killer," *Wall Street Journal*, June 21, 2020, https://www.wsj.com/articles/ george-floyd-and-derek-chauvin-the-lives-of-the-vic tim-and-his-killer-11592761495.

25 "About IFYC," Interfaith Youth Core, https://ifyc. org/about.

26 Eboo Patel and Mary Ellen Giess, "Bring Muslims, Evangelicals, and Atheists Together on Campus," *Chronicle of Higher Education*, November 3, 2015, https://www.chronicle.com/article/Bring-Muslims-Evangelicals/234018.

27 "Be the Bridge," Facebook, https://www.facebook. com/groups/BetheBridge/.

28 Gregg County Elections, "Joint/General Election," November 8, 2016, https://results.enr.clarityelection s.com/TX/Gregg/64736/184366/Web01/en/summ ary.html.

29 "Bridge Construction Methods," WSP, https:// www.wsp.com/en-US/services/bridge-construction-methods.

30 "Brooklyn Bridge," History Channel, https://www. history.com/topics/landmarks/brooklyn-bridge.

31 "Ponte Vecchio," Visit Florence, https://www.visitflo rence.com/florence-monuments/ponte-vecchio.html.

32 Serenitie Wang and Andrea Lo, "How the Nanjing Yangtze River Bridge Changed China Forever," CNN, August 2, 2017, https://www.cnn.com/style/article/nanjing-yangtze-river-bridge-revival/index.html.

33 "White House Honors Atorod Azizinamini," FIU Research, http://research.fiu.edu/2015/12/white-house-honors-atorod-azizinamini/.

Part I   Forging a Path Toward Reconciliation

1 Maxine Najle and Robert P. Jones, "American Democracy in Crisis: The Fate of Pluralism in a Divided Nation," Public Religion Research Institute, February 19, 2019, https://www.prri.org/research/american-democracy-in-crisis-the-fate-of-pluralism-in-a-divided-nation/.

2 Juliana Menasce Horowitz, Anna Brown, and Kiana Cox, "Race in America 2019," Pew Research Center, April 9, 2019, https://www.pewsocialtrends.org/wp-content/uploads/sites/3/2019/04/Race-report_updated-4.29.19.pdf.

3 Andrew Romano, "New Yahoo News/YouGov Poll: Support for Black Lives Matter Doubles as Most Americans Reject Trump's Protest Response," Yahoo News, June 11, 2020, https://news.yahoo.com/new-yahoo-news-you-gov-poll-support-for-black-lives-matter-doubles-as-most-americans-reject-trumps-protest-response-144241692.html.

Chapter 1   From Blindness to Sight

1 Martin Luther King, Jr., "'I Have a Dream,' Address Delivered at the March on Washington for Jobs and Freedom," August 28, 1963. Text available

at Stanford University's The Martin Luther King, Jr. Research and Education Institute, https://king institute.stanford.edu/king-papers/documents/i-ha ve-dream-address-delivered-march-washington-jobs-and-freedom.

2 "CTTT Board of Managers," Coming to the Table, http://comingtothetable.org/about-us/meet-cttt-boa rd/.

3 Daniel Lazarus, et al., "The Project Gutenberg EBook of Moby Dick; or The Whale, by Herman Melville," Project Gutenberg, December 25, 2008, https://www.gutenberg.org/files/2701/2701-h/2701-h.htm#link2HCH0045.

4 Guy Itzchakov and Avraham Kluger, "The Listening Circle: A Simple Tool to Enhance Listening and Reduce Extremism among Employees," *Organizational Dynamics*, vol. 46, issue 4, October–December 2017, 220–226, http://doi.org/10.1016/j.orgdyn.20 17.05.005.

5 Jennifer Levitz, Erin Ailworth, and Tawnell D. Hobbs, "George Floyd and Derek Chauvin: The Lives of the Victim and His Killer," *Wall Street Journal*, June 21, 2020, https://www.wsj.com/articles/georg e-floyd-and-derek-chauvin-the-lives-of-the-victim-and-his-killer-11592761495.

6 "Fatal Force," *Washington Post*, June 14, 2020, https://www.washingtonpost.com/graphics/investi gations/police-shootings-database/.

7 Ibid.

8 "Controversial Police Encounters Fast Facts," CNN, June 4, 2020, https://www.cnn.com/2015/04/05/us/ controversial-police-encounters-fast-facts/index. html.

9 Christina Carrega, "After Breonna Taylor's Death, a Look at Other Black Women Killed During Police Encounters," ABC News, June 6, 2020, https:// abcnews.go.com/US/breonna-taylors-death-bl

ack-women-killed-police-encounters/story?id=710
57133.

10 Katie Wedell, et al., "George Floyd Is Not Alone. 'I
Can't Breath' Uttered By Dozens in Fatal Police
Holds Across US," *USA Today*, June 13, 2020,
https://www.usatoday.com/in-depth/news/investi
gations/2020/06/13/george-floyd-not-alone-dozens-
said-cant-breathe-police-holds/3137373001/.

11 Catherine Rentz, "Hate, Interrupted: Coming to the
Table Offers a Way to Talk About Race," *Baltimore
Sun*, January 21, 2019, https://www.baltimoresun.
com/maryland/anne-arundel/bs-md-coming-to-the-
table-20190121-story.html.

12 Rachael Pacella, "Caucus of African American
Leaders Call for Anne Arundel Schools to 'Proactively
Address Racism,'" *Capital Gazette*, April 10, 2018,
https://www.capitalgazette.com/news/schools/ac-
cn-race-county-schools-0411-story.html.

13 Sara Fischer, "*Axios* Media Trends," *Axios*, July
21, 2020, https://www.axios.com/newsletters/axio
s-media-trends-d14d7aa7-b160-4449-b01d-447b83
fa18e5.html.

Chapter 2   From Human to Human

1 Emily A. King, "Trees of Reconciliation," *Minnesota
Women's Press*, 2017, https://womenspress.com/
Content/Features/Featured/Article/Trees-of-recon
ciliation/1/233/4393.

2 Ruch Clegg, "Sister Cities: Seedbed for the
Grassroots of U.S.–Japan Relations," Sasakawa
Peace Foundation, May 23, 2018, https://spfusa.
org/research/sister-cities-seedbed-for-the-grassroots-
of-u-s-japan-relations/.

3 Jenny Chayabutr, "Request for City Council

Committee Action from the Department of Inter-
governmental Relations," Minneapolis, Minnesota,
July 21, 2009, http://www.minneapolismn.gov/
www/groups/public/@council/documents/webconte
nt/convert_277079.pdf.
4 "Trump Travel Ban: What Does This Ruling Mean?"
BBC News, June 26, 2018, https://www.bbc.com/
news/world-us-canada-39044403.
5 "Cultural, Personal, and Professional Exchanges
Between Minnesota and Iraq," Iraqi and American
Reconciliation Project, https://reconciliationproject.
org/people-to-people.

Chapter 3   From Hating to Healing

1 "Daughters of Zion Cemetery," City of Charlottesville, Virginia, https://www.charlottesvill
e.org/departments-and-services/departments-h
-z/neighborhood-development-services/historic
-preservation-and-design-review/historic-resource
s-committee/local-markers/daughters-of-zion-cemet
ery.
2 Matt Zapotosky, "Charleston Church Shooter: 'I
Would Like to Make It Crystal Clear, I Do Not
Regret What I Did,'" *Washington Post*, January
4, 2017, https://www.washingtonpost.com/world/
national-security/charleston-church-shooter-i-would-
like-to-make-it-crystal-clear-i-do-not-regret-what
-i-did/2017/01/04/05b0061e-d1da-11e6-a783-cd3
fa950f2fd_story.html.
3 WVIR, "Charlottesville City Council Votes to
Rename Lee, Jackson Parks," NBC 29, June 5,
2017, https://www.nbc29.com/story/35595559/cha
rlottesville-city-council-votes-to-rename-lee-jackson
-parks.
4 Chris Suarez, "Charlottesville City Council

Votes to Remove Statue From Lee Park," *Roanoke Times*, February 7, 2017, https://www. roanoke.com/news/virginia/charlottesville-city-council-votes-to-remove-statue-from-lee-park/arti cle_ddbba555-fae0-59da-8997-78a34c97f718. html.

5 "History and Gardens of Court Square Park," City of Charlottesville, Virginia, http://www.char-lottesville.org/departments-and-services/depart ments-h-z/parks-recreation/parks-trails/city-parks/ justice-park-formerly-known-as-jackson-park/his tory-and-gardens-of-justice-park.

6 Phil McCausland, "White Nationalist Leads Torch-Bearing Protesters Against Removal of Confederate Statue," NBC News, May 14, 2017, https://www. nbcnews.com/news/us-news/white-nationalist-leads-torch-bearing-protesters-against-removal-con federate-statue-n759266.

7 Eliott C. McLaughlin, "Charlottesville Rally Violence: How We Got Here," CNN, August 14, 2017, https://www.cnn.com/2017/08/14/us/charlott esville-rally-timeline-tick-tock/index.html.

8 "Rabbi Tom Gutherz's Remarks and Prayer," Charlottesville Clergy Collective, July 11, 2017, https://www.cvilleclergycollective.org/blog/rabbi-tom-gutherzs-remarks-and-prayer.

9 WVIR-TV, "Charlottesville Clergy Collective Marches Ahead of Unite the Right Rally," NBC 29, August 12, 2017, http://www.nbc29.com/story/ 36122315/charlottesville-clergy-collective-marches-ahead-of-unite-the-right-rally.

10 Ibid.

11 Washington Post Staff, "Deconstructing the Symbols and Slogans Spotted in Charlottesville," *Washington Post*, August 18, 2017, https://www. washingtonpost.com/graphics/2017/local/charlottes ville-videos/.

12 Maev Kennedy, "Heather Heyer, Victim of Charlottesville Car Attack, was Civil Rights Activist," *Guardian*, August 13, 2017, https://www. theguardian.com/us-news/2017/aug/13/woman-kil led-at-white-supremacist-rally-in-charlottesville-na med.

13 Gianluca De Fazio, "John Henry James in Albemarle: Racial Terror: Lynching in Virginia," James Madison University, May 17, 2017, https:// sites.jmu.edu/valynchings/va1898071101/

14 Ibid.

15 Tom Gutherz, "The Ark Is Carrying Us: A Reflection from Charlottesville, One Year Later," Religious Action Center of Reform Judaism, August 7, 2018, https://rac.org/blog/2018/08/07/ark-carrying-us-reflection-charlottesville-one-year-later.

16 Ibid.

17 Ibid.

Part II   Reconnecting with Truth

1 William Feuer, "Google Hits an All-Time High as Investors Shrug off Antitrust Investigations," CNBC, January 6, 2020, https://www.cnbc.com/ 2020/01/06/google-and-facebook-hit-all-time-high s-despite-antitrust-probes.html.

2 Carmen Reinicke, "Tech Giants Facebook and Amazon Notch All-Time Highs in Intraday Trading," *Business Insider*, May 20, 2020, https:// markets.businessinsider.com/news/stocks/facebook-and-amazon-stock-prices-hit-all-time-highs-202 0-5-1029221049.

3 "The Fact Checker," *Washington Post*, September 3, 2020, http://washingtonpost.com/graphics/poli tics/trump-claims-database/?itid=lk_inline_manual_ 4.

4 Nathan Bomey, "Parler, MeWe, Gab Gain Momentum as Conservative Social Media Alternatives in Post-Trump Age," *USA Today*, November 11, 2020, https://www.usatoday.com/story/tech/2020/11/11/parler-mewe-gab-social-media-trump-election-facebook-twitter/6232351002/.

Chapter 4   From Fiction to Fact

1 Daniel Funke, "Fact-Checking 'Plandemic': A Documentary Full of False Conspiracy Theories about the Coronavirus," *Politifact*, May 7, 2020, https://www.politifact.com/article/2020/may/08/fact-checking-plandemic-documentary-full-false-con/.
2 Alex Kaplan, "A Coronavirus Conspiracy Theory Film Attacking Vaccines has Racked up Millions of Views and Engagements on YouTube and Facebook," *Media Matters*, May 7, 2020, https://www.mediamatters.org/coronavirus-covid-19/coronavirus-conspiracy-theory-film-attacking-vaccines-has-racked-million-views.
3 Alex Kaplan, "QAnon Conspiracy Theory Post about the Coronavirus Is Spreading on Social Media," *Media Matters*, March 24, 2020, https://www.mediamatters.org/coronavirus-covid-19/qanon-conspiracy-theory-post-about-coronavirus-spreading-social-media.
4 Ibid.
5 Nathan Bomey, *After the Fact: The Erosion of Truth and the Inevitable Rise of Donald Trump*, Prometheus Books, 2016.
6 Ruth Igielnik, "Most Americans Say they Regularly Wore a Mask in Stores in the Past Month; Fewer See Others Doing It," Pew Research Center, June 23, 2020, https://www.pewresearch.org/fact-tank/2020/

06/23/most-americans-say-they-regularly-wore-a-mask-in-stores-in-the-past-month-fewer-see-others-doing-it/.

7 Christopher Ingraham, "New Research Explores how Conservative Media Misinformation may have Intensified the Severity of the Pandemic," *Washington Post*, June 25, 2020, https://www.washingtonpost.com/business/2020/06/25/fox-news-hannity-coronavirus-misinformation/.

8 "Novel Coronavirus(2019-nCoV) Situation Report – 13," World Health Organization, February 2, 2020, https://www.who.int/docs/default-source/coronaviruse/situation-reports/20200202-sitrep-13-ncov-v3.pdf.

9 Kevin Roose, "We Asked for Examples of Election Misinformation. You Delivered," *New York Times*, November 4, 2018, https://www.nytimes.com/2018/11/04/us/politics/election-misinformation-facebook.html.

10 Chengcheng Shao, et al., "Hoaxy: A Platform for Tracking Online Misinformation," in Proceedings of the 25th International Conference Companion on World Wide Web (2016): 745–750, https://doi.org/10.1145/2872518.2890098.

11 Sam Wineburg and Sarah McGrew, "Lateral Reading: Reading Less and Learning More When Evaluating Digital Information," Stanford History Education Group Working Paper No. 2017-A1, October 6, 2017, http://dx.doi.org/10.2139/ssrn.3048994.

12 Amy Mitchell, et al., "Many Americans Say Made-up News is a Critical Problem that Needs to be Fixed," Pew Research Center, June 5, 2019, https://www.journalism.org/2019/06/05/many-americans-say-made-up-news-is-a-critical-problem-that-needs-to-be-fixed/.

13 "Strategic Framework," News Literacy Project,

October 2019. https://www.paperturn-view.com/
us/news-literacy-project/final-strategic-framework-
fy20-web?pid=NTk59804&v=5.

14 Karrie Karahalios, "Algorithm Awareness," MIT
Technology Review, October 21, 2014, https://
www.technologyreview.com/2014/10/21/170668/
algorithm-awareness/.

15 These five TikTok videos are all available on the
MediaWise YouTube channel: "Are Chinese hospitals refusing to treat patients to reduce new
COVID-19 case numbers?" https://youtu.be/Fxobt
M4_fEc; "Does vaping protect you from COVID-
19?" https://youtu.be/JPxfRFhhF6Y; "Did Chinese
doctors confirm African people are immune to the
coronavirus?" https://youtu.be/ZV-CsQtcL4E; "Are
these blacklight images of bacteria on hands legit?"
https://youtu.be/0Sz8tH1OBKA; "Can children
transmit the coronavirus?" https://youtu.be/wRt9R
f7Z2-E.

16 Mack Lamoureux, "People Tell Us How QAnon
Destroyed Their Relationships," Vice, July 11,
2019, https://www.vice.com/en_us/article/xwnjx4/
people-tell-us-how-qanon-destroyed-their-relation
ships.

17 "We Have Met the Enemy and He Is Us," Billy
Ireland Cartoon Library & Museum, https://library.
osu.edu/site/40stories/2020/01/05/we-have-met-the-
enemy/.

18 Alan C. Miller, Twitter, @alanmillerNLP, July 3,
2020, https://twitter.com/alanmillernlp/status/1279
053825136046083.

Chapter 5   From Caricature to Nuance

1 John Saward, "Welcome to Trump County, USA,"
Vanity Fair, February 24, 2016, https://www.vani

tyfair.com/news/2016/02/donald-trump-supporters-west-virginia.

2 Kyle Smith, "Why 'White Trash' Americans Are Flocking to Donald Trump," *New York Post*, July 30, 2016, https://nypost.com/2016/07/30/why-white-trash-americans-are-flocking-to-donald-trump/.

3 Chris Arnade, "Life in Appalachia: Walmart, Church, Politics, and a Tight Community – in Pictures," *Guardian*, September 7, 2016, https://www.theguardian.com/us-news/gallery/2016/sep/07/appalachia-photos-walmart-church.

4 Skye Gould and Rebecca Harrington, "7 Charts Show Who Propelled Trump to Victory," *Business Insider*, November 10, 2016, https://www.businessinsider.com/exit-polls-who-voted-for-trump-clinton-2016-11.

5 Tim Marema, email interview, February 19, 2019.

6 Julia Duin, "In W.Va., Snake Handling Is Still Considered a Sign of Faith," *Washington Post*, November 10, 2011, https://www.washingtonpost.com/lifestyle/magazine/in-wva-snake-handling-is-still-considered-a-sign-of-faith/2011/10/18/gIQAmiqL9M_story.html.

7 Jeffrey Gottfried and Michael Barthel, "Black, Hispanic and White Adults Feel the News Media Misunderstand them, but for Very Different Reasons," Pew Research Center, June 25, 2020, https://www.pewresearch.org/fact-tank/2020/06/25/black-hispanic-and-white-adults-feel-the-news-media-misunderstand-them-but-for-very-different-reasons/.

8 "100 Days in Appalachia," *100 Days in Appalachia*, https://www.100daysinappalachia.com/100-days-in-appalachia/.

9 Dana Coester, "We Ask a Muslim-Appalachian with Kurdish Roots Her Response to Immigration Ban," *100 Days in Appalachia*, January 28, 2017, https://www.100daysinappalachia.com/2017/01/28/ask

-muslim-appalachian-kurdish-roots-response-immi
gration-ban/.

10 "Muslim in Appalachia: Sara Berzingi," *100 Days
in Appalachia*, Facebook video, February 8, 2017,
https://www.facebook.com/100DaysInAppalachia/
videos/1395758470495624/.

11 Jane Stump, "'Who's Next?': Biracial, LGBT College
Student Joins Hundreds to Protest Immigration
Ban," *100 Days in Appalachia*, January 31, 2017.
https://www.100daysinappalachia.com/2017/01/
whos-next-biracial-lgbt-college-student-joins-hun
dreds-protest-immigration-ban/.

12 Molly Born, "LGBTQ Teens Start New Tradition
with West Virginia's First 'Rainbow' Prom,"
100 Days in Appalachia, April 16, 2018, https://
www.100daysinappalachia.com/2018/04/16/lgbt
q-teens-start-new-tradition-with-west-virginias-firs
t-rainbow-prom/.

13 Dave Mistich, "West Virginia's Teacher Walkout
Will Continue for a Third Day," *Salon*, February
26, 2018, https://www.salon.com/2018/02/26/wes
t-virginias-teacher-walkout-will-continue-for-a-thir
d-day_partner/.

14 David Haynes, "Why the *Milwaukee Journal
Sentinel* Replaced Opinion Content with Solutions
Journalism," *American Press Institute*, October 30,
2019, https://www.americanpressinstitute.org/publ
ications/reports/strategy-studies/why-the-milwauke
e-journal-sentinel-replaced-opinion-content-with-
solutions-journalism/.

15 Ibid.

16 Ibid.

17 Edmund Lee and Ben Smith, "*Axios* Allows Its
Reporters to Join Protests," *New York Times*, June
8, 2020, https://www.nytimes.com/2020/06/08/busi
ness/media/axios-allows-reporters-protest-march.ht
ml.

Chapter 6   From Misunderstanding to Understanding

1 Peter DiCampo, "Everyday Africa – Chapter 1, Revisited," https://www.peterdicampo.com/everyday-africa-chapter-1-revisited.
2 Ibid.
3 Noreen O'Donnell, "Students Focus Cameras on Bronx's Bright Sides," *Wall Street Journal*, May 22, 2014, https://www.wsj.com/articles/students-focus-cameras-on-bronxs-bright-sides-1400808881.
4 "2015 Charlie Hebdo Attacks Fast Facts," CNN, December 24, 2018, https://www.cnn.com/2015/01/21/europe/2015-paris-terror-attacks-fast-facts/index.html.
5 Saeed Ahmed and Catherine E. Shoichet, "3 Students Shot to Death in Apartment Near UNC Chapel Hill," CNN, February 11, 2015, https://www.cnn.com/2015/02/11/us/chapel-hill-shooting/index.html.
6 "EverydayRefugees," Instagram, https://www.instagram.com/everydayrefugees/.
7 "EverydayAmericanMuslim," Instagram, https://www.instagram.com/everydayamericanmuslim/.
8 Ben Zimmer, "Is Bezos's 'Complexifier' a Word?" *Wall Street Journal*, February 8, 2019, https://www.wsj.com/articles/a-blackmail-charge-highlights-jeff-bezoss-complexifier-11549641462.
9 Elle Hunt, "New Algorithm-Driven Instagram Feed Rolled Out to the Dismay of Users," *Guardian*, June 7, 2016, https://www.theguardian.com/technology/2016/jun/07/new-algorithm-driven-instagram-feed-rolled-out-to-the-dismay-of-users.
10 "EverydayAfrica," Instagram, http://instagram.com/everydayafrica.

Part III   Redrafting the Blueprint of Compromise

1 Elaine Karmarck and Alexander Podkul, "The 2018 Primaries Projects: The Ideology of Primary Voters," Brookings Institution, October 23, 2018, https://www.brookings.edu/research/the-2018-primaries-project-the-ideology-of-primary-voters/.
2 Norm Ornstein, "Yes, Polarization Is Asymmetric – and Conservatives Are Worse," *Atlantic*, June 19, 2014, https://www.theatlantic.com/politics/archive/2014/06/yes-polarization-is-asymmetric-and-conservatives-are-worse/373044/.
3 Michael Dimock, Carroll Doherty, and Jocelyn Kiley, "Political Polarization in the American Public," Pew Research Center, June 12, 2014, https://www.people-press.org/wp-content/uploads/sites/4/2014/06/6-12-2014-Political-Polarization-Release.pdf.
4 Dan Kahan, "What You 'Believe' About Climate Change Doesn't Reflect What you Know; It Expresses *Who You Are*," Cultural Cognition Project at Yale Law School, April 23, 2014, http://www.culturalcognition.net/blog/2014/4/23/what-you-believe-about-climate-change-doesnt-reflect-what-yo.html.
5 Susan Page, "Divided We Fall? Americans See our Angry Political Debate as 'A Big Problem,'" *USA Today*, December 9, 2019, https://www.usatoday.com/story/opinion/2019/12/05/backstory-america-divided-how-usa-today-help/2599103001/.

Chapter 7   From Denying to Believing

1 "Attention Republican Patriots Ready to Take Back the U.S. Senate!" Sea Island Republican Women, September 14, 2014, https://seaislandrepublican

women.wordpress.com/2014/09/14/attention-re
publican-patriots-ready-to-take-back-the-u-s-sena
te/.
2 Bob Inglis, "Coming to the Realization that We're
All in this Together," republicEn, August 27, 2018,
https://www.republicen.org/events/1-majority-of-
college-of-charleston-students-attending-climate-
keynote-acknowledge-climate-solutions-and-the-
need-to-act.
3 Ibid.
4 Ibid.
5 Jon Ward, "Bob Inglis Wanted to 'Destroy' Bill
Clinton During the 98 Impeachment. Years Later He
Tracked Him Down to Apologize," *Long Game* pod-
cast, December 6, 2019, https://podcasts.apple.com/
us/podcast/bob-inglis-wanted-to-destroy-bill-clin
ton-during-98/id1248994688?i=1000458844222.
6 Nathan Bomey, *After the Fact: The Erosion of
Truth and the Inevitable Rise of Donald Trump*,
Prometheus Books, 2018.
7 "Everything You Need to Know about Coral
Bleaching – and How We Can Stop It," World Wild-
life Fund, https://www.worldwildlife.org/pages/eve
rything-you-need-to-know-about-coral-bleaching-a
nd-how-we-can-stop-it.
8 Cary Funk and Meg Hefferon, "U.S. Public Views
on Climate and Energy," Pew Research Center,
November 25, 2019, http://pewresearch.org/scie
nce/2019/11/25/u-s-public-views-on-climate-and-en
ergy/.
9 "Remarks to the Students and Faculty at Fallston
High School in Fallston, Maryland," Ronald
Reagan Presidential Library & Museum, December
4, 1985, https://www.reaganlibrary.gov/research/sp
eeches/120485a.
10 Ibid.
11 "Cutting the Cord," *The Economist*, October 7,

1999, https://www.economist.com/special-report/
1999/10/07/cutting-the-cord.

12 Psalm 24:1 (King James Version), https://www.bibl
gateway.com/passage/?search=Psalm+24&version
=KJV.

13 Psalm 19:1 (New International Version), https://
www.biblegateway.com/passage/?search=Psalm+19
%3A1&version=NIV.

14 Genesis 1:26 (King James Version), https://www.
biblegateway.com/passage/?search=Genesis+1&ver
sion=KJV.

15 Mark 12:31 (New International Version), https://
www.biblegateway.com/passage/?search=Mark+12%3A28-
31&version=NIV.

16 Funk and Hefferon, "U.S. Public Views."

Chapter 8   From Rigidity to Flexibility

1 Matthew Dolan, "Record Bankruptcy for Detroit,"
Wall Street Journal, July 19, 2013, https://www.
wsj.com/articles/SB1000142412788732399380457
8614144173709204.

2 Nathan Bomey, *Detroit Resurrected: To Bankruptcy
and Back*, W.W. Norton & Co., 2016.

3 Ibid.

4 Ibid.

5 Mark Memmott, "Detroit Is Eligible for Bankruptcy
Protection, Judge Rules," NPR, December 3, 2013,
https://www.npr.org/sections/thetwo-way/2013/
12/03/248357115/detroit-is-eligible-for-bankruptc
y-protection-judge-rules.

6 Paige Williams, "Drop Dead Detroit," *New Yorker*,
January 27, 2014, https://www.newyorker.com/ma
gazine/2014/01/27/drop-dead-detroit.

7 Michael Jackman, "Report Finds Greater Detroit
among Most Segregated US Metropolitan Areas,"

Metro Times, May 25, 2018, https://www.metrot imes.com/news-hits/archives/2018/05/25/report-fin ds-greater-detroit-among-most-segregated-us-metro politan-areas.

8 "QuickFacts: Livonia City, Michigan," US Census Bureau, https://www.census.gov/quickfacts/fact/tab le/livoniacitymichigan/PST045217.

9 "QuickFacts: Detroit City, Michigan," US Census Bureau, https://www.census.gov/quickfacts/detroitci tymichigan.

10 "Detroit And Livonia Rank at the Bottom of Nation for Diversity, Says Report," *Daily Detroit*, May 12, 2016, http://www.dailydetroit.com/2016/05/12/ comes-diversity-study-says-detroit-livonia-rank-bot tom/.

11 "City of Detroit Proposal for Creditors," City of Detroit, June 14, 2013, https://www.documentcloud. org/documents/713693-detroit-emergency-manager -kevyn-orrs-report-to.html

12 David Shepardson, "Gerald Rosen: Architect of the 'Grand Bargain,'" *Detroit News*, November 5, 2015, https://www.detroitnews.com/story/news/ michigan/michiganians-of-year/2015/11/05/michiga nians-year-gerald-rosen-us-district-court-chief-judg e-grand-bargain-architect/75261916/.

13 Monica Davey, "Finding $816 Million, and Fast, to Save Detroit," *New York Times*, November 8, 2014, https://www.nytimes.com/2014/11/08/us/find ing-816-million-and-fast-to-save-detroit.html.

14 Jonathan Oosting, "Michigan House Approves $195 Million for Detroit 'Grand Bargain' Bankruptcy Deal," *MLive*, May 22, 2014, https://www.mlive.co m/lansing-news/2014/05/michigan_detroit_grand_ bargain.html.

15 Bomey, *Detroit Resurrected*.

Chapter 9   *From Discord to Collaboration*

1 1 Kings 3:16–28 (New International Version), https://www.biblegateway.com/passage/?search=1+Kings+3%3A16-28&version=NIV.
2 Timothy Hedeen and Patrick G. Coy, "Community Mediation and the Court System: The Ties that Bind," *Conflict Resolution Quarterly*, vol. 17, 2007, http://doi.org/10.1002/crq.3890170407.
3 Justin R. Corbett and Wendy E. Corbett, "The State of Community Mediation," National Association for Community Mediation, 2011, https://c.ymcdn.com/sites/www.nafcm.org/resource/resmgr/State_of_Community_Mediation.pdf.
4 "Form 990, Return of Organization Exempt from Income Tax," National Conflict Resolution Center, 2017.
5 Kim Werner, "Choose Mediation for Your Divorce: Mediation Costs Less," National Conflict Resolution Center, https://www.ncrconline.com/divorce-family-law-mediation-articles/choose-mediation-your-divorce-mediation-costs-less.
6 Laura Rena Murray, "How Arbitration Clauses Silence Women Speaking Out About Harassment," *Vice*, November 30, 2017, https://www.vice.com/en_us/article/ywnzmj/how-arbitration-clauses-silence-women-speaking-out-about-harassment.
7 Alexander J. S. Colvin, "The Growing Use of Mandatory Arbitration," Economic Policy Institute, April 6, 2018, https://www.epi.org/publication/the-growing-use-of-mandatory-arbitration-access-to-the-courts-is-now-barred-for-more-than-60-million-american-workers/.
8 Kate Hamaji, "Justice for Sale: How Corporations Use Forced Arbitration to Exploit Working Families," Center for Popular Democracy, May 2017.

https://populardemocracy.org/sites/default/files/Forc
ed-Arbitration_web%20(3)_0.pdf.

9 "About Us," National Conflict Resolution Center,
https://www.ncrconline.com/mediation-conflict-res
olution/about-ncrc.

10 "Galinson Campus Civility Program," National
Conflict Resolution Center, https://www.ncrconline.
com/sites/default/files/pdfs/ncrc-fund-dev-civility-f.
pdf.

11 "Knight Foundation/Gallup First Amendment
Survey," Knight Foundation, December 2017, https://
kf-site-production.s3.amazonaws.com/media_eleme
nts/files/000/000/148/original/2017_Knight_Found
ation_First_Amendment_Survey_Topline_1_.pdf.

Conclusion

1 John M. Bridgeland and John J. DiIulio, Jr., "Will
America Embrace National Service?" Brookings
Institution, October 2019, https://www.brookings.
edu/wp-content/uploads/2019/10/National-Service_
TEXT-3.pdf.

2 "Inspired to Serve: Executive Summary," National
Commission on Military, National, and Public Ser
vice, March 2020, https://inspire2serve.gov/sites/def
ault/files/final-report/Executive%20Summary.pdf.

3 Bridgeland and DiIulio. "Will America Embrace
National Service?"

4 Isabel Sawhill and John Bridgeland, "Here's a Cost-
Effective National Service Proposal that Could Bridge
our Deep Divisions," Washington Post, February 21,
2020, http://washingtonpost.com/opinions/2020/02/
21/heres-cost-effective-national-service-proposal-tha
t-could-bridge-our-deep-divisions/.

5 Kimberly Amadeo, "FY 2020 Federal Budget
Compared to Actual Spending," The Balance,

November 6, 2020, https://www.thebalance.com/
fy-2020-federal-budget-summary-of-revenue-and-s
pending-4797868.

6 Sawhill and Bridgeland, "Here's a Cost-Effective
National Service Proposal."

7 Nick Anderson, "Should Colleges Let Students
Choose their First Roommate? Some Say No,"
Washington Post, June 11, 2018, https://www.was
hingtonpost.com/local/education/should-colleges-let
-students-choose-their-first-roommate-some-say-no/
2018/06/10/bd2a1d1a-4edf-11e8-af46-b1d6dc0d9b
fe_story.html.

8 Ibid.

9 Jeremy Bauer-Wolf, "Random Roommates Only,"
Inside Higher Ed, March 2, 2018, https://www.
insidehighered.com/news/2018/03/02/duke-universi
ty-blocks-students-picking-their-roommates-freshm
an-year.

10 Anderson, "Should Colleges Let Students Choose
their First Roommate?"

11 Bauer-Wolf, "Random Roommates Only."

12 Ibid.

13 Jason Grumet, "Promoting Civility, Collaboration,
and Bipartisanship in Congress," Bipartisan Policy
Center, September 26, 2019, https://bipartisanpoli
cy.org/letter/promoting-civility-collaboration-and-b
ipartisanship-in-congress/.

14 Ibid.

15 "About the Caucus," Problem Solvers Caucus, https://
problemsolverscaucus-gottheimer.house.gov/about.

16 Andrew Restuccia, Burgess Everett, and Heather
Caygle, "Longest Shutdown in History Ends after
Trump Relents on Wall," *Politico*, January 25,
2019, http://politico.com/story/2019/01/25/trump-s
hutdown-announcement-1125529.

17 "Inaugural Address of John F. Kennedy," Yale Law
School Lillian Goldman Law Library's The Avalon

Project, January 20, 1961, https://avalon.law.yale.
edu/20th_century/kennedy.asp.

18 Yale Law School Lillian Goldman Law Library, "First
    Inaugural Address of Abraham Lincoln," March 4,
    1861,   https://avalon.law.yale.edu/19th_century/lin
    coln1.asp.